# The ABA Guide to

# LAWYER
# Trust Accounts

## by Jay G Foonberg, J.D., CPA

with annotations by Ellen Peck, Esq.

**ABA** Section of Law Practice Management

Library of Congress Catalog Card Number 96-85887

ISBN 1-57073-360-0

00 99 98 97 96   5 4 3 2 1

Discounts are available for books ordered in bulk. Special consideration is given to state bars, CLE programs, and other bar-related organizations. Inquire at Publications Planning and Marketing, American Bar Association, 750 N. Lake Shore Drive, Chicago, Illinois 60611.

# CONTENTS

# ABOUT THE BOOK

I decided to write this book because there is a need for it. I have observed that few if any lawyers receive any formal training or education in *how* to manage client trust accounts to comply with ethical and statutory requirements. Teaching materials, if they exist, are often imprecise. These materials were developed to fill that gap.

Lawyers are often entrusted with large amounts of client funds without training in the processing of those funds. Lawyers and clients both suffer when the lawyer is not trained to avoid the problems that can lead to professional and financial disaster for both. It is unfortunate that many Certified Public Accountants (CPAs) with law firm clients are unfamiliar with statutory ethical requirements. Many lawyers depend on the CPA to know what has to be done while the CPA is depending on the lawyer to know what has to be done. The resulting gap can spell trouble for both professionals.

The questions commonly asked of me by attendees at my Ethics and Loss Prevention and Management seminars clearly reflect that lawyers are not adequately prepared for their ethical responsibilities.

The existing literature is confusing and often directed more at punishing erring lawyers or preserving interest income for bar activities than at protecting clients' funds or teaching lawyers or law students what to do and how to do it. I hope this book will fill the gap in the existing teaching materials.

This book takes a more conservative or "better safe than sorry" approach. Some of my conclusions and recommendations are stricter than what is required in a specific jurisdiction. One who resolves questions with no clear solutions or answers available will be less likely to get in trouble by using the recommendations set forth in this book.

Information found in one section is sometimes repeated in part in another section. This allows the reader or lecturer or other user to touch upon a point rather than treat it extensively. The lecturer or reader can cover the points desired to be covered in a class or session of one hour or less. This format allows the user to read only one or two sections in a few minutes and benefit from the few minutes spent.

This book is designed as a national book for law school and continuing legal and professional education courses and individuals throughout the United States. It will generally be accurate wherever it is used. Lecturers are encouraged to add handouts or supplements reflecting special local rules or modifications or giving additional special emphasis to recent or current developments in a particular state at a particular time.

This book is intended to be used for the following:

- A permanent reference book for the lawyer's personal library
- Course materials for a continuing legal education (CLE) course in ethics or law practice management for practicing lawyers
- Course materials for a one-hour law school lecture as part of a course in professional responsibility for law students
- Course materials for a one-hour course in trust accounts as part of a "Bridging the Gap" course for new lawyers.
- A teaching guide and reference work for bookkeepers, office managers, paralegals, secretaries, and others in law firms who deal with the receipt of monies and the processing of legal matters
- A guide for CPAs with lawyer clients
- A guide and reference work for bankers with lawyer clients
- A one-hour self-study course for lawyers in states that allow self-study. A written examination is included for that purpose.
- A self-study course for minor violators of IOLTA or other trust account rules
- A companion book for law students to a case book on professional responsibility

The book is divided as follows:

**1. Text.** The text portrays typical and common trust account problems faced by practicing lawyers in a law practice. It is factual and not state-specific. The sections are "stand-alone" so the lecturer or user may omit selected sections without affecting the remaining sections the lecturer or user may wish to discuss or study in greater detail.

**2. Sample Forms.** Sample form letters and reports are included to be modified and used by a law firm. The lecturer or user may add state-specific or other rules, cases, and the like if desired.

**3. Where to Find Help.** The lawyer or student is encouraged to compile a list of trust account resources available where he or she practices, or will practice, law. This list can be prepared by the lecturer as additional course material if desired.

**4. Self-Test.** This section can be used as an "open book" test to be turned in by the lawyer or student and then graded if desired. The lecturer can indicate which questions the lecturer wishes answered or omitted.

**5. IOLTA (Interest on Lawyers' Trust Accounts).** IOLTA rules are technically not ethics rules, but exist in every state. An appendix with a list of IOLTA authorities is included for reference.

# ABOUT THE AUTHOR

Jay G Foonberg is a lawyer who lives in Beverly Hills, California, and practices in Santa Monica. He is also a licensed CPA in California. He is the author of many articles and books and has contributed to numerous publications on lawyer marketing, client relations, law office management, and law office accounting. He has been assisting law students and new lawyers for more than three decades in Bridging the Gap Seminars, Law School Lectures, and private and bar-sponsored Continuing Legal and Professional Education seminars.

Mr. Foonberg based this book on his hands-on experiences with thousands of new and experienced lawyers who have attended his seminars and, through their questions, demonstrated their need for this information.

A graduate of UCLA and UCLA Law School, Mr. Foonberg has served the legal and accounting professions in many capacities. His innovative contributions include serving as a founder of the American Bar Association Law Practice Management Section, founder and chair of the ABA New Lawyers in Practice Committee, founder and president of the American Association of Attorney–Certified Public Accountants, founder and chair of the State Bar of California Law Practice Management Section, and founder and chair of the Inter-American Bar Association Law Practice Management Committee.

He is also the founder and president of the National Academy of Law, Ethics & Management, Inc. (NALEM), a nonprofit society for the advancement of the art of teaching the interdisciplinary relationship of law, ethics, and management. NALEM has worked with bar organizations, bar counsel, bar-related insurance companies, private firms, CLE organizations, and universities in its effort to reduce disciplinary and malpractice claims through education and training in the fields of law office management and client relations.

He has been honored with the ALI-ABA Consortium's Harrison Tweed Award for lifetime achievements in teaching law office management in every state of the United States and for books and articles and presentations. He is also a recipient of the Louis Goldberg Award as the Most Outstanding Attorney-CPA in the United States. Mr. Foonberg is a Charter Fellow of the College of Law Practice Management.

Among his other books available from the ABA are *Finding the Right Lawyer, How to Start and Build a Law Practice* (now in its third edition), and *How to Get and Keep Good Clients.*

# A NOTE TO
# THE LAW FIRM'S CPA

This book concerns your client's license to practice law. It would be helpful for you to read this publication and the local rules concerning client trust accounts to help your client install and maintain accounting and internal control systems to comply with the rules. Innocent errors can cost your client time, money, and embarrassment and result in disciplinary proceedings—even though your client did not intentionally violate the rules.

Your client's reliance on you may or may not mitigate any discipline for violating the rules, but it will not relieve your client of any responsibilities and may not be found to be a justified reliance.

Do not rely on generally accepted accounting principles to apply with respect to lawyers' client trust accounts.

The law governing attorney-client duties can be found in the law of fiduciaries, the law of principal and agent, and trust law. Unfortunately, the generally accepted accounting theories and terminology relative to fiduciary accounting, trust accounting, and the presentation of financial information are not always applicable to lawyers' client trust accounting.

In some situations, the disciplinary authorities will accept your commonsense reconciliations, terminology, procedures, and presentations of information. In some situations, the disciplinary authorities will insist that everything be done their way, with their terminology, etc., even if their way bears no relationship to the world of public accounting. You must take special care to help prevent improper commingling. For example, I recommend omitting the client trust accounts from the financial statements. You should read the applicable client trust account rules with the same care and approach you would read tax rulings or the rules promulgated by your state board of accounting.

A typical regulation concerning trust account records is included at the end of Part I ("Typical State Rules Concerning Records"). I recommend you read it to get a feeling for the types of information required and the sometimes unique vocabulary used by legal boards in describing accounting records.

The legal profession is deeply concerned with protecting client money, and Interest on Lawyers' Trust Accounts (IOLTA) authorities are deeply concerned about getting all the interest they can from the lawyer's trust account. Accordingly, the rules are often written to protect these concerns rather than to protect the lawyer or to provide the lawyer with useful information for financial management purposes.

Please read this book carefully and obtain and study a set of the applicable rules to best help your client with trust account procedures and management.

# ACKNOWLEDGMENTS

Many people and institutions have been instrumental in demonstrating the need for this book and helpful in formulating the problems and the solutions. Of special note are many of the individual members of the National Organization of Bar Counsel who personally reviewed drafts of the materials and offered comments. These individuals reflected the opinion that education of lawyers and law students and CPAs is important to reduce rule violations.

Lawyers Mutual Insurance Company of California and several other bar-related malpractice insurance companies, including companies in Missouri, Wisconsin, Kansas, and Alabama, encouraged the inclusion of trust account management in the client relations seminars I did for them or in their states. Willis Baughman of Lawyers Mutual Insurance Company of California and David Harding of the Bar Plan in Missouri were most supportive and helpful in the paying of my expenses in presenting CLE programs.

The State Bar of Nevada and its disciplinary counsel and CLE staff were most helpful in allowing me to teach their annual one-hour mandatory ethics course and to use that course to concentrate on trust account problems and solutions. Leonard Gang, Stan Peyton, Rob Bare, and Cathie Olendorff were most supportive.

The Honorable Ellen Peck of the California Bar Court spent many hours arguing problems and solutions. Many of the problems presented are from actual disciplinary cases. Judge Peck has prepared the endnotes that appear in this edition.

Several members of the American Bar Association Section of Law Practice Management encouraged this book and reviewed it.

Robert Conroy of New Jersey and Gary Munneke of New York went far beyond the call of duty in their efforts.

Several law practice management advisors were helpful in presenting the need for these materials. J.R. Phelps of the Florida Bar Law Office Management Assistance Program, Nancy Wilson of the Oregon Bar, and Steven Gallagher of the New York State Bar Association offered comments and support over the years.

Most importantly I wish to acknowledge Steven Mark Foonberg of the National Academy of Law, Ethics & Management, Inc., for his exceptional efforts in organizing the materials and arranging for distribution of the book and its drafts and the audiotape and videotape versions of these materials.

Last but not least I must thank the literally hundreds of practicing lawyers throughout the United States who confidentially shared their problems with me, offered their experiences, and related their solutions.

# FOREWORD

Most lawyers learn in law school ethics class that the quickest route to disbarment is to "commingle" their funds with client trust funds— that is, to have a single account where the lawyer's money and the client's money are mixed. Few lawyers, however, know the stringent state ethics rules that apply to setting up client trust accounts, keeping appropriate records for those accounts, and properly reporting the disbursement of the funds to their clients. These rules have increased in complexity now that each state requires lawyers to put trust account funds into special accounts that earn interest used by the state bar authorities for such things as reimbursing clients whose trust funds have been misused or funding legal aid activities.

The ABA Section of Law Practice Management is dedicated to providing practical information to help practicing lawyers achieve excellence, provide the highest-quality service to their clients, and avoid professional pitfalls. LPM Publishing, the Section's publishing arm, has brought out a number of titles on quality control, ethics, and risk management topics to aid lawyers in fulfilling their obligations.

Founding LPM member Jay Foonberg's landmark books *How to Start and Build a Law Practice* and *How to Get and Keep Good Clients* have helped tens of thousands of lawyers to succeed in the practice of law. Through years of presenting seminars to lawyers on ethics and management topics, Mr. Foonberg (an attorney and Certified Public Accountant) discovered that lawyers and their accountants have few places to go to learn the mechanics of complying with the ethical rules concerning client trust accounts. *The ABA Guide to Lawyer Trust Accounts* was written to provide that information in a format that is easy to understand and applies to any size and type of legal practice that receives client funds, regardless of your individual state's rules.

Mr. Foonberg has designed the book to be used as a self-study course or as seminar materials, with short, stand-alone chapters that walk you through the procedures of client trust accounting. In his down-to-earth, no-punches-pulled style, Mr. Foonberg gives you the history of the applicable ethics rules, explains how you could inadvertently be violating those rules and exposing yourself to discipline even where no one is harmed, discusses the pitfalls of the Interest on Lawyers' Trust Account (IOLTA) requirements, suggests ways to work with your banker and accountant to set up the office systems you need to avoid trust problems, and provides numerous forms that you can adapt for your office. His "Ten Rules of Good Trust Account Procedures" and "Ten Steps to Good Trust Account Records" are intended to work with whatever local rules your state mandates.

The book also contains a self-test, for the use of seminar instructors and lawyers whose states award continuing legal education credits for self-study courses in legal ethics. The test is intended not as an applied bookkeeping skills demonstration, but to determine whether you recognize the issues, terminology, and procedures concerning client trust accounts, and it is a useful tool for checking your understanding. Your own state's rules will determine whether use of this book qualifies for CLE credit.

The license to practice is the most valuable asset the lawyer owns. LPM Publishing believes that this book should be required reading for every lawyer who wishes to preserve that precious asset.

Robert J. Conroy
Judith L. Grubner
Co-Chairs, LPM Publishing

# PART I

## UNDERSTANDING TRUST ACCOUNT PRINCIPLES

## THE IMPORTANCE OF TRUST ACCOUNT MANAGEMENT

The shortest and most direct road to disbarment or other disciplinary action runs through the client trust account. Trust account complaints and violations are treated seriously and disciplined severely.[1]

When a trust account violation occurs, it is usually easy to prove. The paperwork or lack of paperwork makes it easy to "prosecute" trust account cases. All of the presumptions are against the lawyer, and the burden is on the lawyer to prove innocence.[2] If a lawyer is found "guilty" of a violation, the consequences can be grave. Unintentional and negligent trust account management can result in discipline and civil liability.[3] Intentional trust account mismanagement can result in disbarment, civil liability, and criminal liability.[4]

Most trust account problems are the result of poor management occasioned by lack of knowledge and training. Most trust account problems can be avoided by following simple rules. There is no need for lawyers or law firms to risk their licenses and livelihoods for trust account rules violations.

This book lays out basic principles and procedures to help you avoid violations. As you read each section, keep in mind the purposes of maintaining trust accounts.

## COMMON TRANSACTIONS REQUIRING TRUST ACCOUNTS

Trust accounts are commonly used for a variety of traditional purposes whenever a lawyer is in possession of money that does not belong to the lawyer.

Common examples include the following:

1. Personal injury settlements[1]
2. Real estate closings[2]
3. Collections received for the client in collection and subrogation work[3]
4. Amounts used for dispute settlements[4]
5. Medical payments from the client's medical insurance coverage[5]
6. Advances for costs[6] or fees[7] received from a client or from a third party for the benefit of the client
7. Unearned lawyer's fees including minimum fees not yet earned[8]
8. Deposits to secure payment of lawyer's fees and costs[9]
9. Disputed lawyer's fees pending resolution[10]
10. Funds received for the benefit of nonclient third parties (in some jurisdictions)[11]
11. Client funds to be used for investments or purchases of property[12]
12. Payments of spousal support (alimony) or child support for transmission by or to a lawyer[13]
13. Funds retained from a client's money or settlement to be used to pay liens and assignments made by the client or imposed by operation of law[14]
14. Proceeds of sale of estate properties or trust properties or client properties[15]
15. Funds appropriately and legally entrusted to the lawyer by the client to be used as directed by the client[16] (for example, payments where anonymity is appropriately desired)
16. Any money that does not belong to the lawyer[17]

17. Any money received in connection with the legal representations of a client
18. Any property, especially of value, belonging to a client or third party received in connection with the legal representation of a client (for example, stocks, bonds, jewelry, and works of art)

## HISTORY AND BACKGROUND OF THE ETHICS
## RELATING TO CLIENT TRUST ACCOUNTS

The responsibility of a lawyer to segregate the funds of a client and to account to the client has its origins primarily in the common law of agent and principal. The common law of agency imposes duties on the part of the agent to the principal.

The common law of principal and agent and the common law of fiduciary and beneficiary include the following principles:

- The duty to account to the beneficiary
- The duty to give information to the beneficiary
- The duty to safeguard the property of the beneficiary
- The duty to act with honesty
- The duty of confidentiality
- The duty of good faith

A lawyer's fundamental responsibilities with respect to a client's money and property would not be significantly different if no bar association or state bar or court or legislature had ever adopted any ethical rules.

The creation of ethical or disciplinary rules has simply codified relevant parts of the existing common law of principal and agent for the purpose of giving licensing bodies the standards and the ability to discipline a lawyer for violation of the rules. The client has always had the power to seek civil or criminal redress without reference to the disciplinary rules or disciplinary authorities.

The first step toward codification in America occurred in 1836, when David Hoffman of the Baltimore Bar wrote "50 Resolutions in Regard to Professional Deportment." During the 1850s, Judge George Sharswood of Pennsylvania used these fifty resolutions in a series of lectures at the University of Pennsylvania and collected the lectures as a series called "The Aims and Duties of the Profession of Law." In 1887, Thomas Goode Jones of Alabama took David Hoffman's fifty resolutions as modified by Judge Sharswood and put them together as the Alabama Code of Ethics. In 1908, the American Bar Association, at its first Annual Meeting, copied the Alabama Code of Ethics and called it the American Bar Association Canons of Professional Ethics.

Just as the American Bar Association copied the Alabama Bar Association's pronouncements, many state, federal, and local disciplinary authorities have copied in whole or in part the American Bar Association's pronouncements.

However, many states have refused to follow, copy, or be bound by significant portions of the American Bar Association canons. The ABA itself has made several major overhauls of its rules. Accordingly, in citing any authority for an ethical opinion one must be careful to remember that each disciplinary authority has its own rules, which might be identical, similar, or contrary to the rules of the ABA or any other disciplinary body.

For this reason, this book teaches generally applicable principles of trust account management rather than a detailed list of specific bookkeeping requirements or a list of specific rules and interpretations.

## DIFFERING ABA AND STATE RULES

So the reader can observe the differences between the trust account rules of differing disciplinary bodies, presented here is the historical development of trust account principles within the American Bar Association and the principles of one state, California.

## Differing ABA Rules

The ABA's concepts are not binding on any lawyer anywhere. The ABA has no authority to discipline any lawyer. Authorities can and do totally disregard the position of the ABA and decide ethical issues in an opposite manner.

The ABA's rules and interpretations nonetheless have value because they are often adopted in whole or in part and are often looked to for general guidance. When there is a serious problem, it is often helpful to be aware of the ABA position and history and to compare and contrast that position and history to the rules being applied to the specific situation. Here is a summary of some major developments.

1. In 1908, at its first Annual Meeting the American Bar Association copied the ethical provisions of the Alabama Bar Association and called the result the American Bar Association Canons of Professional Ethics. Included in the Canons was Canon 11, which read in part:

> Money of the client or collected for the client or other trust property coming into the possession of the lawyer should be reported and accounted for promptly, and should not under any circumstances be commingled with his own or be used by him.

2. In 1970, the ABA replaced the Canons of Professional Ethics with the American Bar Association Model Code of Professional Responsibility. Included under the framework of the new Code was Disciplinary Rule 9-102, which, under "Preserving Identity of Funds and Property of a Client," read

> (A) All funds of clients paid to a lawyer or law firm, other than advances for costs and expenses, shall be deposited in one or more identifiable bank accounts maintained in the state in which

the law office is situated and no funds belonging to the lawyer or law firm shall be deposited therein except as follows:

    (1) Funds reasonably necessary to pay bank charges may be deposited therein.

    (2) Funds belonging in part to a client and in part presently or potentially belonging to the lawyer or law firm must be deposited therein, but the portion belonging to the lawyer or law firm may be withdrawn when due unless the right of the lawyer or law firm to receive it is disputed by the client, in which event the disputed portion shall not be withdrawn until the dispute is finally resolved.

    (B) A lawyer shall:

    (1) Promptly notify a client of the receipt of his funds, securities, or other properties.

    (2) Identify and label securities and properties of a client promptly upon receipt and place them in a safe deposit box or other place of safekeeping as soon as practicable.

    (3) Maintain complete records of all funds, securities, and other properties of a client coming into the possession of the lawyer and render appropriate accountings to his client regarding them.

    (4) Promptly pay or deliver to the client as requested by a client the funds, securities, or other properties in the possession of the lawyer which the client is entitled to receive.

3. In 1983 the ABA replaced the Model Code of Professional Responsibility with the American Bar Association's Model Rules of Professional Conduct. Included in the new Model Rules is Rule 1.15, which reads

    (A) A lawyer shall hold property of clients or third persons in connection with a representation separate from the lawyer's own property. Funds shall be kept in a separate account maintained in the state where the lawyer's office is situated, or elsewhere with the consent of the client or third person. Other property shall be identified as such and appropriately safeguarded. Complete records of such account funds and other property shall be kept by the lawyer and shall be preserved for a period of years after the representation.

(B) Upon receiving funds or other property in which a client or third person has an interest, a lawyer shall promptly notify the client or third person. Except as stated in this rule or otherwise permitted by law or by agreement with the client, a lawyer shall promptly deliver to the client or third person any funds or other property that the client or third person is entitled to receive and, upon request by the client or third person, shall promptly render a full accounting regarding such property.

(C) When in the course of representation a lawyer is in possession of property in which both the lawyer and another person claim interests, the property shall be kept separate by the lawyer until there is an accounting and severance of their interest. If a dispute arises concerning their respective interests, the portion in dispute shall be kept separate by the lawyer until the dispute is resolved.

## Differing State Rules

California Rule 4-100 is typical of many state bar rules and is repeated here. Most states and various other disciplinary authorities have their own versions of what is or is not considered "ethical" or "professional," and these versions may from time to time differ from each other and from the ABA. Purely as an example: the California version mandates inclusion of advanced costs and expenses in the trust account; Washington, D.C.'s rules expressly state that advances for costs become the property of the lawyer upon receipt;[1] and New York's trust account rule is silent.[2] Again, one must always be knowledgeable of the rules of a particular state.

Rule 4-100. Preserving Identity of Funds and Property of a Client

(A) All funds received or held for the benefit of clients by a member or law firm, including advances for costs and expenses, shall be deposited in one or more identifiable bank accounts labelled "Trust Account," "Client's Funds Account" or words of similar import, maintained in the State of California, or, with the written consent of the client, in any other jurisdiction where there is a substantial relationship between the client or the client's business and the other jurisdiction. No funds belonging to the member or the law firm shall be deposited therein or otherwise commingled therewith except as follows:

(1) Funds reasonably sufficient to pay bank charges.

(2) In the case of funds belonging in part to a client and in part presently or potentially to the member or the law firm, the portion belonging to the member or law firm must be withdrawn at the earliest reasonable time after the member's interest in that portion becomes fixed. However, when the right of the member or law firm to receive a portion of trust funds is disputed by the client, the disputed portion shall not be withdrawn until the dispute is finally resolved.

(B) A member shall:

(1) Promptly notify a client of the receipt of the client's funds, securities, or other properties.

(2) Identify and label securities of a client promptly on receipt and place them in a safe deposit box or other place of safe-keeping as soon as practicable.

(3) Maintain complete records of all funds, securities, and other properties of a client coming into the possession of the member or law firm and render appropriate accounts to the client regarding them; preserve such records for a period of no less than five years after final distribution of such funds or properties; and comply with any order of such records issued pursuant to the Rules of Procedure of the State Bar.

(4) Promptly pay or deliver, as requested by the client, any funds, securities, or other properties in the possession of the member which the client is entitled to receive.

(C) The Board of Governors of The State Bar shall have the authority to formulate and adopt standards as to what "records" shall be maintained by members and law firms in accordance with subparagraph (B) (3). The standards formulated and adopted by the Board, as from time to time amended, shall be effective and binding on all members.

In addition, although Interest on Lawyers' Trust Accounts (IOLTA) is technically not part of the ethics rules governing lawyers, it is a significant source of income to bar organizations. The relatively recent zealous enforcement of trust account ethics rules seems to coincide with the relatively recent arrival of IOLTA. Since IOLTA violations are reported to bar authorities, and the bar authorities react with disciplinary investigations, it is important to include IOLTA with trust accounts although theoretically and technically IOLTA is independent of ethics. IOLTA is covered in separate sections of this book.

## A SUMMARY OF COMMON-LAW BACKGROUND AND ORIGINS OF TRUST ACCOUNT RULES

Trust account rules are not arbitrary rules created to earn money for bar foundations through IOLTA laws, nor are they rules created to set up unwary lawyers to be disciplined or disbarred.

Most ethics rules concerning the maintenance of trust accounts arise out of the common-law principals of the law of agency and from the common law of trusts. Some of the rules developed out of the law of assignments.[1] In an extremely oversimplified fashion, the following summary may be helpful in understanding the reasons for the trust account rules. Legal scholars may debate some of the conclusions contained in this simplified and generalized explanation, but for our purposes this explanation is accurate enough.

1. Under the principles of agency law, the relationship between a lawyer and a client is that a lawyer is an agent and a client is a principal.[2]

2. When the acts of the agent (the lawyer) fall within the scope of employment, the relationship becomes a fiduciary-beneficiary relationship, with the lawyer becoming the fiduciary and the client becoming the beneficiary.[3]

3. When there is a fiduciary (the lawyer) and a beneficiary (the client) and money or property is added to the formula, the money or property becomes the res or principal (not to be confused with the principal in a principal-agent relationship) and there is a trust, since by definition the elements of a trust are the presence of a fiduciary, a beneficiary, and a res.[4]

4. In some cases involving third parties, the third party becomes an assignee or a third-party beneficiary pursuant to an agreement between the client and the third party[5] (liens for medical services being a common example).

5. Some of the common-law duties of a fiduciary (agent) to a beneficiary (principal) include the following:

- The duty to account to the beneficiary[6]
- The duty to give information to the beneficiary[7]

- The duty to act with honesty[8]
- The duty to safeguard the property of the beneficiary[9]
- The duty of confidentiality[10]
- The duty to act with utmost good faith[11]

In many situations, questions concerning trust accounts can be answered by reference to the law of agency or the law of trusts. The law of agency and the law of trusts are often good starting points in answering questions not anticipated by the rules.

## INTEREST ON LAWYERS' TRUST ACCOUNTS (IOLTA)

Every state has some form of system to obtain the interest that lawyers' trust accounts could otherwise earn for clients.[1] The system is sometimes called IOLTA, an acronym for Interest on Lawyers' Trust Accounts, and sometimes IOTA, for Interest on Trust Accounts, or IOLA, for Interest on Lawyers' Accounts.

The interest is used for various purposes depending on the state. In some cases it is used to protect clients when a lawyer steals client trust money. In some cases it is used to fund legal aid. There are many different uses to which the money is put, depending on the enabling act.

Typically, the state bar or other organization has entered into a contract with one or more banks wherein the bank is approved for IOLTA and the bank pays a negotiated rate of interest at negotiated times to the state bar or other organization.

Before the institution of IOLTA, lawyers often kept clients' money in non-interest-bearing trust accounts. Often the amount of money being deposited and the short time the money was in the bank made it impractical for the lawyer to open separate accounts for every matter and then to compute interest on a daily basis and then send that interest to the clients. It was easier and more practical to keep the money in a non-interest-bearing checking account unless large amounts of interest were involved. The banks were often happy to have these interest-free deposits, and often gave the lawyer favorable amounts or favorable interest rates on office working capital loans or sent business to the lawyer to say "thank you." Those days are over, and the trust accounts now bear interest and the interest goes to the state bar or other organization. Outside of the United States, it is still a practice in many countries for law firms to keep for themselves the interest earned on their clients' funds.

Typically the bank will have a contract with the state bar or other organization, the terms of which will become part of the lawyer's contract with the bank.

There are four things you have to know about the IOLTA system where you practice or intend to practice.

1. Where to get a copy of the IOLTA rules. A list of addresses is included in Appendix D.

2. Whether the bank you want to use is approved for IOLTA.
3. Whether the bank has a "snitch rule" agreement with the state bar.
4. When not to use IOLTA.

## When Not to Use IOLTA

IOLTA accounts are only intended to be used when the amount of interest that could be earned by a client in a separate interest-bearing account is not justified by the time and energy involved[2] (for example, getting the client's Social Security or Employer Identification Number and filing IRS Form 1099, Information Return, on the client).

If a significant amount of interest could be earned for the client, then you should open a separate interest-bearing account for the matter and be sure the client(s) gets the interest.[3]

As an example, I will relate what happened to me. An estate had just sold some real estate (the home of the decedent) and was ready to close. I received a check for the estate from the real estate broker, believing the distribution to the heirs would occur in a week or so. One of the heirs objected to the sale and asked for a court hearing, which was granted. The hearing was postponed several times at the request of the heir. When the hearing was finally held, the probate judge was angry at the heir for wasting the court's time and threw the case out. The same heir then moved to surcharge my fee by the amount of interest the account would have earned had I set up a non-IOLTA interest-bearing account. Another probate judge, hearing the matter, agreed with the heir, even though the heir was the cause of the delay, and the judge reduced my fees by $4,000, the amount of interest IOLTA got that the estate didn't get. The judge suggested I seek a refund from IOLTA, which I did. As you might guess, IOLTA refused to pay any part of the surcharge to offset my losses for the money that IOLTA received.

Be sure you understand that interest earned on trust accounts should not always go to IOLTA.[4] The right of clients to the interest on their funds may be superior to the right of IOLTA to interest,[5] and you may be in the middle.

When the disposition of or the right to trust account funds is in dispute, the amount of money and time needed to resolve the dispute may be significant. If there is likely to be a significant or substantial amount of interest to be earned, it may be prudent to remove the money from the IOLTA account and put it in a non-IOLTA account where the interest can accumulate for the benefit of the person ultimately entitled to the trust account funds.[6]

In some jurisdictions, non-IOLTA trust accounts must be placed in a bank,[7] while IOLTA accounts may be placed in other types of financial and nonfinancial institutions approved by the local IOLTA authorities[8] (for example, savings and loans, credit unions, and even private individuals).

## The IOLTA Snitch Rule

It is critical and perhaps even urgent that you understand that many banks have a "snitch rule" (sometimes called a "reporting rule"), which obligates them as part of their contract to notify the state bar or government agencies of any bounced checks, in or out, or any other irregular transactions.[9] Fault is not an issue. The bank will snitch to the state bar even when the bank made the error. The result may be an unannounced surprise visit and full-blown audit of your trust account for a three-year period. Even though you are totally exonerated of any fault or responsibility concerning the transaction that led to the snitch, other problems from other years can be uncovered.

I have been told many horror stories about banks that made mistakes, erroneously crediting a trust account deposit to a wrong account and then bouncing a trust account check. For example, a bank's computers reported the bounced check to IOLTA. The lawyer sent in a complete explanation, including two affidavits from the bank and a letter of apology from the bank and documents from the client substantiating that the client's check was honored on redeposit. All to no avail. The IOLTA auditor came out, did a three-year audit, and found several violations that had occurred when the office had an office manager who had been fired for bank reconciliation mistakes. The end result was a full hearing and a reproval and a lot of lost time and money for the lawyer involved.

A typical snitch rule can be found in the California Business and Professions Code at Section 6091.1:

> . . . a financial institution . . . shall report to the State Bar in the event any properly payable instrument is presented against an at-

torney trust account containing insufficient funds, irrespective of whether or not the instrument is honored.

The state bar may then issue a secret subpoena for trust account records without prior or contemporaneous notification to the lawyer, who will be informed thirty days after the records have been turned over.[10]

Accordingly, be sure you understand the nature and extent of the snitch rule and be very careful to choose a competent bank if you have any options. Simply having a friendly banker or bank manager may not be enough. The notices of the disciplinary authorities are often generated by computers and sent out with no human being in the process. Bank competence is important.

A large number of the reports to bar disciplinary authorities are simply the result of the lawyer issuing checks against the funds before the funds are officially credited and the checks are honored and, while no one is aware of the technical violation, the notice goes out from the bank's computers to the disciplinary authorities because of the technical violation.

## NO DELEGATION OF TRUST ACCOUNT RESPONSIBILITY

Any lawyer who is in day-to-day charge of a matter must understand that he or she has trust account responsibility for that matter. That lawyer, to protect himself or herself, should have a separate trust account for those matters under that lawyer's responsibility. If the firm's partners are worried, the account can require two lawyers' signatures on checks. Larger firms may have more accounting procedures and safeguards, but human error or dishonesty can occur in any size firm.

- A lawyer cannot avoid trust account responsibility by delegating the maintenance of the trust account to a bookkeeper, office manager, or "managing partner"[1] or to any other person or institution.
- A sole practitioner cannot avoid responsibility by delegating the trust account maintenance to his or her sole assistant.
- A lawyer in a small- or medium-size firm cannot avoid responsibility by delegating the trust account maintenance to the office manager.
- A lawyer in a large firm cannot avoid responsibility by delegating the trust account maintenance to the managing partner and the bookkeeper.
- A lawyer in a mega-firm cannot avoid responsibility by delegating the trust account maintenance to the director of finance or the head of computer and accounting support services.
- A partner in a large firm can be held financially liable and be professionally disciplined for intentional and negligent trust account management by others in the firm.
- A lawyer can be disciplined for failure to properly supervise and review the activities of those who maintain trust accounts and trust account refunds.
- A lawyer can be disciplined for failure to properly supervise the activities of an outside management firm that failed to properly supervise its employees.

The foregoing examples, although some overlap, clearly make the point that firm size is no insulation from trust account responsibility.

It is incumbent upon the lawyer in charge of a matter to stay close to that matter and personally be involved in approving and/or reviewing all trust account transactions as to that matter. The managing partner or the bookkeeper may resent the "interference" into the firm's operations, but that is simply the price lawyers must pay to be sure the client is protected.

If you are an associate or junior partner who is denied access to the accounting records by firm management, you should put your concerns in writing and be sure the management committee or the senior partner in the firm gets the memo. You have to be assertive to protect your license to practice and the client's money. You may wish to expand the distribution of the memo to all partners, along with a notation that all partners in the firm may have vicarious disciplinary and financial responsibility if something goes wrong with the trust account.

In some law firms, every lawyer in the firm has a separate trust account upon which only that lawyer can sign.

Do not allow the bookkeeper or office manager or outside accountant or any other third person to sign checks;[2] do not use a rubber endorsement stamp or mechanical or computer-generated signatures; and do not pre-sign blank checks.[3] It's your license to practice law.

## A LAWYER CAN BE DISCIPLINED EVEN IF NO ONE IS "HURT"

There is no "no harm, no foul" rule in the arena of trust accounts.[1]

- A lawyer can be disciplined for failure to segregate funds even though the client promptly receives all funds due the client.[2]
- A lawyer can be disciplined for unreasonable delay in returning or paying or depositing trust account funds even though the client eventually receives every penny to which the client is entitled.[3]
- A lawyer can be disciplined for "borrowing" the money from the trust account for a few hours or a few days even though everyone receives every penny to which they are entitled.[4]
- A lawyer can be disciplined for being technically "out of trust" even though everyone promptly receives their money.[5]
- A lawyer can be disciplined for inadvertently allowing the funds of one client to be used to pay another client due to a bounced check that wasn't the lawyer's "fault."[6]
- A lawyer can be disciplined for failure to deposit funds to the trust account that should have gone to the trust account even though no client suffered from the delay.[7]
- A lawyer can be disciplined for failure to maintain the records required even though no client lost a penny or suffered any delay in receiving funds.[8]
- A lawyer can be disciplined for failure to have the required records segregated and available for immediate inspection even though there are no financial irregularities.[9]
- A lawyer can be disciplined for failure to properly safeguard trust account records.
- A lawyer can be disciplined for poor training, poor management, or poor supervision of the nonlawyer staff involved with trust accounts.[10]
- A lawyer can be disciplined for failure to properly supervise and review the activities of outside management firms.
- A lawyer can be disciplined for poor supervision of other lawyers in the firm with respect to trust accounts and trust moneys even though no client ever lost a penny.[11]

- A lawyer can be disciplined for the trust account acts or omissions of partners even though no one lost any money.[12]
- A lawyer can be disciplined for failure to produce trust account records[13] even though there have not been any financial improprieties.
- A lawyer can be disciplined for failure to properly use a client trust account even though the lawyer has acted pursuant to the affected client's written instructions and consent.[14]

The trust account arena is not the basketball arena, and the disciplinary court is not the basketball court. There is no "no harm, no foul" rule in the world of trust accounts.

## THE MECHANICS OF A TRUST ACCOUNT INVESTIGATION

It may be helpful to know how trust account investigations begin, how they are conducted, what the investigators look for, and what happens as a result of the investigation.

While there are differences from investigator to investigator and jurisdiction to jurisdiction, what is described here is relatively typical.

### Why the Investigation Is Commenced

*A purely random audit.* A state bar number is picked out of a hat or computer list and the auditor writes a letter or shows up at the door. This scenario in fact happens, but it is extremely rare.[1]

*A complaint from a client.* A client complains to the state bar that the lawyer said the case was settled but the lawyer hasn't sent the client any money. This is a common beginning point.

Another common complaint from a client is that the client paid the fee in advance and the lawyer hasn't done the work and won't refund the fee. Since unearned fees are supposed to go to the trust account, there may be a trust account investigation as to whether the fees ever were deposited to the trust account and what subsequently happened.

*A complaint from a disgruntled former spouse or former employee.* These revenge complaints are often relegated to the bottom of the pile, but eventually they do get investigated.

*A complaint from a third party.* A client has promised money to a third party out of money that will go through the trust account, and has executed a lien form giving the third party a lien on the money. The third party knows or believes the money has arrived and wants the lien honored. When no money is forthcoming, the third party goes to the state bar and complains. This is a common beginning point, especially in those states that give third parties the same trust account status a client gets.

*Snitches from banks under IOLTA agreements.* The term "snitch" is offensive to some people, but it is in fact the terminology commonly used. "Reporting Rules" or "Mandatory Reporting Rules" would be another way of describing the requirements. Many states have an agreement with banks approved for IOLTA deposits that requires the bank to report any irregularity regardless of who caused the irregularity and regardless of whether the irregularity or problem was straightened out to everyone's satisfaction.[2] A lawyer asked the author for help when the lawyer's bank erroneously credited a trust account deposit to another customer's account, causing a check issued by the lawyer to bounce. The bank's computer reported the bounced check to the State Bar even though the lawyer was totally ignorant of what was happening and had done nothing wrong. The bank on discovering its error sent profuse letters of apology to the client, the lawyer, and the state bar. The state bar felt it had no choice, under its procedural rules, but to do a full three-year trust account audit. The state bar subpoenaed the bank's records and did a three-year audit, discovering two negligent situations that had occurred two years previously. The lawyer received a reprimand for the earlier negligence even though the lawyer was completely exonerated on the matter of the bank mistake. IOLTA interest money is like any other governmental money. At first it's found money, then the organization becomes dependent on the money. Some professional responsibility lawyers erroneously believe that IOLTA audits go up as interest rates go down.

*A snitch from another lawyer.* Most states have some form of snitch rule requiring lawyers to snitch on other lawyers when a trust account violation is observed or suspected.[3] Some lawyers will snitch even when there is no snitch rule requiring them to snitch. Most lawyers would snitch only if they saw or suspected repeated violations. Some lawyers file complaints to get some perceived advantage.

*Referrals from judges.* Judges and bankruptcy referees often file a complaint based on what they see in their courtrooms.[4]

*The Internal Revenue Service (IRS) and other government and police agencies.* The IRS often suspects lawyers of leaving fees in a trust account beyond December 31st in an attempt to report the income from a matter in a subsequent tax year, thereby deferring the taxes. Other government agencies may suspect a lawyer's trust account is being used for money laundering or disguising political campaign contributions or bribes or for some other illegal purpose.

*"Aggressive stupidity."* It is a sad fact that every year lawyers throughout America pay bar association dues, convention registration fees, and continuing legal education (CLE) enrollments with client trust account checks. Bar personnel are alerted to look for and report these situations.

## What Happens During the Audit[5]

The auditor may or may not notify the lawyer when there is an impending audit. The auditor may go directly to banks or third parties and subpoena or request records without informing the lawyer of what is happening. The lawyer may be kept unaware of what is happening until after the records have been delivered. This will not enhance the lawyer's public image even if it should be determined that the lawyer is totally faultless.

At some point the auditor will contact the lawyer and ask for the lawyer's trust account records, bank statements, and cancelled checks and deposit tickets for a three-year period. The auditor may or may not ask for specific client files showing calculations of fees, divisions of funds, and the like.

If the auditor is sophisticated, he or she will have a computer program to reconstruct the trust records from the documents. It should be kept in mind that the auditor could reconstruct most of what he or she needs purely from the subpoenaed records of third parties even if the lawyer claims the lawyer's records are lost or destroyed or unavailable.

Note that failure to properly maintain and have available trust account records may be a disciplinable offense even if the trust account has always been perfectly in balance.

The auditor will reconstruct the following records:

1. Trust account cash receipts journal
2. Trust account cash disbursements journal
3. Specific client ledgers (for specific matters)
4. Schedule of client balances (all clients accounts taken together)

The auditor will reconstruct the records two different ways:

1. Using the lawyer's handwritten or typed entry dates as being accurate

2. Ignoring the lawyer's handwritten or typed dates and using the dates the items were posted by the banks

The resulting computer-generated reports will clearly show if any client accounts or if all client accounts in the aggregate were out of trust and on exactly which date or dates or periods of time they were out of trust.

More importantly, the resulting computer reports will show if being out of trust was the result of an occasional honest mistake or negligence or whether there was a pattern of consistently being out of trust.

## What Happens After the Audit

If it appears that the lawyer was occasionally out of trust as the result of honest mistake or negligence, the lawyer may or may not receive a private or public reprimand or reproval. (A lawyer can be disciplined for innocent or unintentional violation of trust account rules.)

If it appears that the lawyer was consistently, repeatedly, or deliberately out of trust, it may be time to say good-bye to the license to practice law for a fixed or indeterminate period of time—or permanently.

## TYPICAL STATE RULES CONCERNING RECORDS

Various state bar authorities and IOLTA authorities require records to be kept in a certain way and to include certain information.[1]

Unfortunately, there is no uniformity from state to state as to the requirements[2] or the vocabulary used to describe what is wanted. The same records are often given differing names. The same word often describes differing records.

The problem is further complicated by the fact that there is not necessarily any connection between generally accepted accounting practices and what is required. The vocabulary used to describe what is required may bear no relation to the vocabulary used in the world of business or the world of accounting.

The rules promulgated by the Board of Governors of the State Bar of California are included here as a typical set of state rules and as a general reference point to the vocabulary used and the types of records and reports one state demands. Do not assume that these rules or the rules of any one state will apply in whole or in part anywhere else. It is imperative that local rules containing local vocabulary and local requirements be obtained and studied.

A member shall, from date of receipt of client funds through the period ending five years from the date of appropriate disbursement of such funds, maintain:

(a) A written ledger for each client on whose behalf funds are held that sets forth

(i) the name of such client,

(ii) the date, amount, and source of all funds received on behalf of such client,

(iii) the date, amount, payee, and purpose of each disbursement made on behalf of such client, and

(iv) the current balance for such client.

(b) A written journal for each bank account that sets forth

(i) the name of such account,

(ii) the date, amount, and client affected by each debit and credit, and

(iii) the current balance in such account;

(c) all bank statements and cancelled checks for each bank account, and

(d) each monthly reconciliation (balancing) of (a), (b), and (c).

# PART II

---

# THE BASICS OF
# TRUST ACCOUNT MANAGEMENT

## HAVE A TRUST ACCOUNT

A lawyer can't deposit money to a trust account if the lawyer doesn't have a trust account. Open a trust account under your control as soon as you get your license to practice law even if you don't see an immediate need for a trust account and even if you are with a firm that has one (unless you can sign on the firm's trust account and are willing to be responsible for what the other signatories on the account do with the money you deposit).

The need for a trust account may be sudden and unanticipated. You may receive a large amount of cash and need to deposit it immediately for safekeeping. A client or relative of a client may give you a large retainer in advance or costs in advance that must be deposited immediately. If you don't have a trust account, you might be tempted to deposit the funds to a personal account or to leave them totally unprotected, either of which could leave your license and your assets exposed.[1]

If you don't need the account, you'll have wasted a few dollars in check-printing charges. If you do need it, you'll be glad you have it.

Every law firm should have a client trust account in addition to the usual general office bank account, the client costs advanced bank account, and the payroll bank account. Individuals should have their own personal bank account.

If you are in a firm, consider opening your own client trust account for those cases and clients for which you are responsible. Law firms do go under without prior notice to clients or junior partners and sometimes without prior notice to senior partners. You may be left with a personal trust account responsibility to a specific client. If the firm objects to you having your own client trust account, offer the firm a joint signature control on the account. Your personal assets and your license to practice law may be involved if the firm goes under or if there is a trust account problem on the matters for which you are responsible. The author has personally represented "innocent" law firm partners in state bar and malpractice proceedings, where an errant partner mismanaged the firm trust account. Alcohol, drugs, and marital problems can and do cause partners to take trust account money, leaving "innocent" partners with serious problems. Trust account disciplinary rules apply equally to lawyers in megafirms and lawyers in sole practice.

## WHERE TO OPEN AND KEEP THE TRUST ACCOUNT

In most jurisdictions the local rules or the IOLTA rules require that a trust account be in a bank[1] or other state or federally insured institution[2] located in the state.[3]

The account must normally be in the lawyer's state so IOLTA can get the interest under its banking agreements and so the account is under the subpoena jurisdiction of the state bar disciplinary system.

Multistate law firms must normally maintain the client's trust account in the state where the client is located, if the law firm has an office in that state, or in the state where the responsible lawyer is located. This is to protect the client. Since trust account responsibility is the primary responsibility of the individual lawyer in charge of the matter, the trust account must be in the state where that lawyer has his or her office, regardless of where the headquarters of the law firm might be.

In some cases the client may direct that funds are to be deposited and withdrawn from a bank outside the state or indeed outside the United States.[4] The client may require this for asset protection purposes or for any number of bona fide business or tax reasons. The lawyer will have to determine if an out-of-state or out-of-country trust account is permissible under the applicable rules. If the client wants an offshore trust account, the lawyer should get the instructions in writing and remind the client that there won't be any insurance protection. In some states, an out-of-state account is allowed if the client has some bona fide relationship to that jurisdiction and if the rules concerning insurance are satisfied. In some states, out-of-state trust accounts are prohibited. In some states, an "approved list" is maintained and only institutions or individuals on the list may be used. An out-of-state trust account may be permissible for a specific client in a specific matter, but it would be extremely unlikely that a lawyer could establish and maintain a normal trust account outside the lawyer's state.

In some cases the rules permit an IOLTA account to be in a savings and loan, a credit union, or a brokerage account or other type of thrift institution insured by the state or federal government but require a non-IOLTA trust account to be in a bank.[5] The lawyer must read the rules of the applicable state.

It may be necessary or even preferable to keep trust funds in an institution other than one regularly used by the firm or its partners for their own purposes.

## Federal and State Deposit Insurance

It is prudent funds management that all trust accounts be insured by the federal government against the failure of the financial institution. Banks and savings institutions can and do close Friday afternoon and not reopen Monday morning. The amount of Federal Deposit Insurance Corporation (FDIC) or Federal Savings and Loan Insurance Corporation (FSLIC) insurance may be the only insurance protection that exists. Normally the amount of insurance is $100,000, but that amount is sometimes increased depending on the number of beneficiaries and the interest of each beneficiary. Some states allow the financial institution to be insured by a state insurance agency.

Some states make it mandatory that all funds in the account be adequately insured. Other states allow the lawyer the luxury of guaranteeing the solvency of the bank with the lawyer's license to practice law and his or her personal net worth. Banks can and do close on Friday afternoon and not reopen Monday morning.

If a lawyer is going to put more than $100,000 into a single institution, the lawyer should be sure there is adequate insurance for the amount deposited. If adequate insurance can't be gotten at one bank, spread the deposit around to several institutions where there is adequate insurance.

The lawyer should confirm the coverage in writing with the institution. For example, if the lawyer deposits $50,000 from each of ten clients, be sure there is $500,000 of insurance and all are insured, rather than having $100,000 of insurance and being at risk for $400,000.

If the lawyer or firm is going to receive more than the amount of insurance coverage from a third-party source (for example, an insurance company or buyer of property), the lawyer should either get the funds in $100,000 increments to be deposited in multiple institutions or get a written waiver from the client if permitted by the rules.

It is the author's personal experience that the subject of insurance is sometimes not adequately considered by IOLTA or the disciplinary authorities in their banking agreements or legislation. The legislation sometimes seems more concerned with getting the interest income and punishing the lawyer than protecting the lawyer and the lawyer must take steps independently to be sure there is adequate insurance for each client and each matter. Adequate insurance is often the responsibility of the individual lawyer. Failure to be sure of adequate insurance may or may not be a disciplinary or malpractice problem, depending on the rules of the jurisdiction.

## HAVE A CLIENTS SAFE DEPOSIT BOX OR A FIREPROOF SAFE

A lawyer is required to segregate and protect valuable things that don't belong to the lawyer in addition to money that doesn't belong to the lawyer.[1]

From time to time a lawyer will come into possession of valuable personal property, such as wills, share certificates, original documents, negotiable instruments, jewelry, or other properties, which require segregation and protection.[2]

A lawyer should rent a clients safe deposit box at the most nearby convenient bank for easy access when necessary. This box should be in addition to the firm or personal box.

Lawyers should double-check their theft and fire and comprehensive insurance to be sure there is adequate insurance to cover these items, which are technically owned by the client (*non-owned* in insurance terminology) and therefore possibly noninsured as being excluded items under the terms of the office policy.

In the old days, lawyers had fireproof safes in their offices, but this is no longer common. Many lawyers have fireproof safes in their homes that can serve on a temporary or emergency basis when the bank is closed. As indicated later, a client may permit a lawyer to commingle the lawyer's property and the client's property as opposed to commingling a client's funds with the lawyer's funds.

While most lawyers are familiar with the requirement of having a client trust account for client funds, surprisingly many are unaware of the need for a clients safe deposit box or other secure means to safeguard items that must be protected.

Disciplinary Rule 9-102 (B) (2) of the ABA Model Code of Professional Conduct is typical of similar rules that have existed for many years in most states. That rule reads: "A lawyer shall: . . . Identify and label securities and properties of a client promptly upon receipt and place them in a safe deposit box or other place of safekeeping as soon as possible."

The safe deposit box should clearly be labeled as a "Clients Safe Deposit Box," and should ideally be in addition to the lawyer's own box, and should not contain property or valuables of the lawyer.

Interestingly enough, unlike putting cash funds into an IOLTA account, a client apparently may in some states direct that noncash personal property be kept in a nonsafe place. For example, the client may direct that personal property be kept in a place where its availability rather than its safety is important. Since there is no loss of interest income, there does not seem to be any overwhelming prosecution of lawyers for failure to maintain a safe deposit box properly.

## THE GENERAL RULES OF FEES AND TRUST ACCOUNTS

The transfer of fees into and out of the trust account is complicated, even in routine situations. In complex situations, the transfer of fees into and out of the trust account can be a nightmare for all involved. Well-intentioned, honest errors in judgment can have serious disciplinary and financial consequences for the lawyer involved.

### Earned vs. Unearned Fees—The General Rule

Unearned fees must be deposited to the trust account and kept in the trust account until earned, at which time they must be removed.[1] Until the fees are earned, the money belongs to the client and can even be reached by the client's creditors, by attachment or execution, including a bankruptcy trustee or the government or former spouse. Since the funds belong to the client, you must keep them separate from your funds.

Earned fees must be removed when earned.[2] When the fees are earned, they become your funds and must be kept separate from the client's funds.

Leaving earned fees in the trust account is not only unethical, it is bad business. The IRS will be very upset if you leave your earned fees in the trust account to avoid or defer paying income taxes on the fees. As indicated in the discussion on unearned fees, you may find yourself in a skirmish with creditors or others who want to get the funds when you claim you have earned them as fees. You may be between a rock and a hard place if you have to tell the client's creditors that the funds belong to you and then explain to the disciplinary prosecutors why you haven't taken the earned fees out of the trust account. If you have this dilemma, another lawyer may have to report you under a squeal rule or a judge may report you to the disciplinary authorities.

Lawyers facing disciplinary charges for depositing unearned fees to an office or personal account instead of to a client trust account often assert as a defense that the client directed or consented to the transaction. "Client's consent" or "client's instruction" does not allow a lawyer to deposit unearned fees to anywhere but the trust account and will not be accepted as a defense to a disciplinary charge.[3]

## Nonrefundable Minimum Fee Deposits

The ethics of nonrefundable minimum fees are beyond the scope of this treatment of trust accounts. The subject of nonrefundable fees is controversial and frequently centers on whether a fee is "reasonable" or not under the circumstances. The issue is often whether or not the lawyer has "earned" the fee. Again, some jurisdictions prohibit nonrefundable minimum fees where no work is done beyond accepting the engagement. This is beyond the scope of this book.

Many lawyers insist on nonrefundable minimum fee deposits to protect themselves if the client wants to fire the lawyer or if the lawyer becomes conflicted out of representing the other side due to having listened to the facts. When a lawyer listens to a party's version or perception of the facts, the lawyer has gained confidences of the client and cannot represent an adverse party or violate the client's confidence. This subject is controversial in some states.[4] If the deposit is nonrefundable, it probably should be removed from the trust account as soon as the client's check clears. This area is muddled and in flux and differs greatly in different jurisdictions.[5] You must, however, be aware of the problem and seek help. Retainer fees are covered in another section.

If your client dies or fires you or goes bankrupt, you normally can withdraw fees earned to that point in time. You might have to file a probate claim or bankruptcy claim for future fees unless your fee agreement gives you appropriate protection as a lien or in some other manner.

## Transfer of Fees When Earned

Normally, you may transfer fees to your office account from the trust account when earned without waiting for client approval of the amount of the fees.[6] You must notify the client of the transfer and remaining balance at the time of transfer or at any prompt time agreed to between you and the client, such as on the monthly statement.[7] If the client objects or complains, you must immediately return the amount in dispute to the trust account until the problem is resolved.[8] If you know the fee or part of it is in dispute, it should not be removed from the trust account. (Disputed funds are discussed in other sections.)

## RETAINER FEES AND TRUST ACCOUNTS

The subject of what fees do go into the trust account and what fees don't go into the trust account is complicated because the terminology is not universally the same from lawyer to lawyer or state to state. The subject becomes even more complex when dealing with retainer fees.

The definitions and rules given here might be different from jurisdiction to jurisdiction but are generally technically correct.

1. *Retainers.* The word "retainer" is widely misused by lawyers and disciplinary authorities. A true retainer is the fee charged by a lawyer to secure the services of that lawyer[1] and as a consideration that the lawyer will not be available to represent an adverse or potentially adverse party. For example, after hearing a party's version of the facts of a case, the lawyer would be conflicted out of representing other parties in the case. The retainer fee is the lawyer's fee for being available to the client and not being available to the others.

A true retainer is not an advance payment of a fee or a deposit to ensure payment of future fees. If the client fires the lawyer or never uses the lawyer in the future, the retainer was completely earned at the beginning.

Since a true retainer is earned when paid, it belongs to the lawyer and should not go into the client's trust account.[2]

2. *Deposit.* A deposit to secure payment of fees belongs to the client until earned and accordingly must go into the trust account until earned,[3] at which time the fees must be removed from the trust account as earned fees belonging to the lawyer. A deposit to secure payment of fees represents unearned fees and should not be called a retainer, which is earned fees. Unearned fees, as indicated, must go into the trust account.[4] If the lawyer is fired, the lawyer must return to the client the unearned part.[5]

3. *Advanced Fees.* Advanced legal fees for work not yet performed are of the same nature as the deposit and must go into the trust account until earned, when they can and must be removed.[6]

There may or may not be a difference between a deposit for legal fees and advanced legal fees under debtor-creditor rights, or for income tax treatment, but for trust account purposes they are the same. They must go into the trust account until earned, at which time they must be removed.

4. *Nonrefundable Fees.* A nonrefundable legal fee by any name can be in and of itself unethical in many jurisdictions.[7] The prohibition is more directed to noncriminal consumer situations such as divorce than to corporate situations such as hostile takeovers. One rationale is that getting paid for doing nothing is on its face an unreasonable fee. Another rationale is that a lawyer must promptly refund unearned fees on request of the client. Nonrefundable legal fees still have to go into the trust account.[8]

5. *Minimum Fees.* Minimum fees are generally treated the same way as nonrefundable fees. They must go into the trust account until earned and then must be removed.[9]

6. *Fixed Fees.* A fixed fee must go into the trust account[10] until the work is done. In the event of dispute the lawyer would be able to charge based on common-law principles of contract.

7. *Contingent Fees.* Contingent fees and fees payable from proceeds of settlements, sales, and the like must be removed when the funds are credited, provided your fee agreement allows you to do so. A properly drafted fee agreement will normally allow the lawyer to withdraw nondisputed fees. Without a properly drafted fee agreement, the lawyer may have to give all the money to the client and send a bill to the client hoping to get paid. The subject of contractual and noncontractual lien rights or property rights to lawyer's fees is beyond the scope of this book.

8. *"Retainers" and Fee Agreements.* A lawyer should clearly define in discussions with the client and in the fee agreement exactly what is meant by the word "retainer" or the words "retainer fee." The lawyer would be well-advised to use the words "nonrefundable retainer fee earned when received" or the words "an advance payment of fees to be withdrawn when earned" or similar words to clearly describe what is intended.

## HANDLING CLIENT COSTS

Handling client costs can be a bit complicated. The lawyer must follow trust account rules when a client advances costs and the lawyer must follow trust account rules when reimbursing the firm for client costs advanced.

For purposes of this discussion, "client costs" is defined as being funds expended to third parties. Excluded from this discussion of costs are those charges some law firms call "costs," such as photo reproduction charges or electronic research charges, or other "costs" that are actually charges for the firm's services.

When a client advances anticipated costs on a matter, the lawyer must deposit the money to the client trust account.[1] The funds belong to the client and must be segregated and not commingled. This is basic and fundamental.

It is theoretically good practice to pay all client costs directly from the trust account. As a practical matter it may be better for a firm to advance some smaller and unknown costs from the general or office account and then reimburse that account monthly from the trust account for all costs advanced during the previous month. This system reduces the number of transactions in the trust account and channels overpayment problems to the office account. (It is always critical to remember that if the lawyer inadvertently spends more for a client than is in the account for that client, the lawyer will be improperly using other clients' monies for the one client.) This system also enables the lawyer to report once a month to the client rather than every time a check is written.

In some cases, checks have to be sent to government agencies or private companies for open-ended or indeterminate amounts. These checks are typically written by a lawyer with the words "not to exceed $xxxx" in the number portion and in the word portion of the check. The lawyer may not know the amount of the check until it is returned by the bank with other cancelled checks one or two months later. It is cleaner and easier to use the office account or special cost checking account for this type of expenditure of client funds and then reimburse the firm from the trust account when the amount is known, at which time the client should be notified.

When the firm is reimbursed, the firm must notify the client as it would for any trust account expenditure, either at the time of expenditure or on an agreed periodic bill or statement.

If the firm has advanced costs from the office account and is subsequently reimbursed for those costs, the reimbursement can go directly to the office account if it is clearly distinguishable as reimbursement for the costs expended.[2] If there is a combination of reimbursement and/or advances for future costs or fees, the lawyer should deposit the money into the client trust account[3] and then reimburse from the trust account.

Many law firms maintain a "Client Costs" bank account from which the firm advances client costs and expenses and to which the firm transfers reimbursements from clients and reimbursements from the proceeds of the case for previously expended costs. The lawyer may ethically maintain a "cushion" for future needs without violating any rules because the account is not a client trust account. Naturally client costs advanced by the client prior to expenditure by the lawyer must go to the client trust account. The client costs may then be paid directly from the client trust account.

Client costs advanced by the firm from the firm's money in the client cost account, which is not a trust account, may be reimbursed to this account by the client or from the ultimate recovery in the case.

## CHARGING FEES FOR TRUST ACCOUNT SERVICES

Many large firms charge fees to their clients for trust account transactions, especially in probate and trust matters. A clerical fee is charged for every check, every deposit, every bank reconciliation, every client notification, and so forth. This clerical fee is charged in addition to the lawyers' time involved. This is probably permissible if the client consents in advance, but the lawyer should check local law before charging for trust account transactions, which are ethically required.

## DEALING WITH EXCESS AND UNEXPLAINED FUNDS

In theory, there should never be excess or unexplained funds in the trust account. In reality, it sometimes happens that there is money in the trust account that doesn't belong there for a number of reasons. Common causes of discovery of excess funds include the following:

1. A client disappears and cannot be located to pay the client their share of an award or settlement[1] or the balances due the client for unexpended deposits received for costs.
2. Trust account checks don't get cashed and the outstanding check is included in the reconciliation for years.[2]
3. There is a fee dispute and the client refuses to do anything or reach any agreement as to the funds.
4. A new bookkeeper or CPA does the reconciliations and the unidentified excess cash is "discovered." This frequently occurs when a new partner comes in or the outside auditor wants to get rid of uncashed checks or unexplained differences.
5. A lawyer tries to defer a fee to a subsequent tax year and then is afraid to say anything.
6. Funds were kept to be disbursed at the direction of a client[3] who never gave instructions and now cannot be located.

These situations put the law firm in a quandary. To come forward may result in disciplinary action for failure to maintain a trust account properly. The coming forward would probably mitigate any serious discipline, but the stain on the firm would still be there.

The law firm cannot simply take the money in as fees and pay income taxes on the money. To do so could be an act of conversion or misappropriation of one or more clients' monies.

Additionally, the funds could be subject to the state's escheat laws or unclaimed credits laws.

### Common Solutions

There are several possible options open to the lawyer, depending on the problem and the jurisdiction. The best starting point is to simply come forward and tell the truth. Notify the disciplinary authorities of the excess funds as soon as you discover them and ask for guidance. Consider the following solutions to common problems:

1. Exercise due diligence in locating and communicating with the client. "Due diligence" may be different depending on whether there is $8.40 of unused cost funds or $18,000.00 from a bankruptcy liquidating dividend paid four years after the claim. Due diligence may run from checking phone books, voter rolls, and driver's licenses to hiring a private investigator.

2. If there is an unresolved fee dispute, litigate it or arbitrate it in accordance with your jurisdiction's rules. If possible ask that the award of fees direct that the award may be withdrawn from the trust account. Depending on your right to a lien on the funds, you may have to execute on the funds or you may simply be able to withdraw them from the account.

3. If the amount is large and the source or origin cannot be readily determined, hire an outside auditor to audit the account to determine the source of the funds and who is entitled to them. If the outside auditor cannot make the determination, then presumptively the state bar auditor won't be able to either. You must then decide to assume the funds are yours and take them in as fee income/costs recovered or decide they belong to unknown clients and observe the escheat laws.

4. Review the various statutes of limitations for disciplinary proceedings, malpractice exposure, conversion of client funds, and escheat and then decide on a course of action.

5. Send the money to IOLTA in exchange for its promise to return the money should the rightful owner be discovered or come forward.

6. Pay the money to the state in accordance with the escheat laws.[4]

7. Pay the money into court and file an interpleader or declaratory relief proceeding naming the disciplinary authorities, the IOLTA authorities, and the state attorney general or whoever enforces the escheat laws. (You might even be able to claim and be awarded interpleader fees.)

Do not, under any circumstances, simply take or keep the money for yourself without proper authority for doing so, hoping no one will know. This is risky and not worth the trouble. In many states there is no statute of limitations for ethics violations.

## DEALING WITH SHORTAGES

A shortage may arise due to embezzlement by a bookkeeper or a lawyer. The shortage may arise from a bookkeeping error. The shortage may arise from paying out funds against a deposit that bounced or "held" or was not credited for any reason.

If the lawyer discovers the shortage before the bank does and the lawyer makes up the shortage with no injury to any client, the lawyer might still have an exposure for negligent management of the trust account.[1] If this happens to you, you should determine if your state has any rule requiring you to self-report shortages, even if they are immediately covered with your funds before any harm comes to anyone.

As mentioned previously, there is no "no harm, no foul rule" in most jurisdictions.[2] A determination must be made if there was a bona fide innocent error[3] or if there is a pattern of "borrowing" money from the trust account and replacing it before the client knows. The lawyer may face discipline even for honest error.[4]

## WHAT TO DO WITH DISPUTED AMOUNTS

Disputes over trust account funds can be extremely serious. It is not uncommon for a lawyer in good faith to withdraw fees or other amounts believed to have been earned or payable from the funds and then to have a dispute with the client over the withdrawal.[1]

The lawyer is ordinarily bound to put the money back into the trust account if the client makes a reasonably timed objection.[2] This can be a very serious problem with respect to funds paid to third parties who will not refund them. Some states allow the lawyer to interplead the money, or what's left of it, into court and to litigate.

When the dispute concerns fees, some states have arbitration procedures, which may be either permissible or mandatory.[3]

If the amount of money in dispute is significant or is likely to be in dispute long enough to earn "significant" or "substantial" interest, it may be prudent to transfer the money into a non-IOLTA account where it can earn interest for the client or others ultimately entitled to the money.

It is, of course, far preferable to avoid disputes altogether, a subject covered in other parts of this book.

# PART III

---

# AVOIDING DISPUTES
# OVER TRUST ACCOUNTS

## AVOIDING DISPUTES

The best way to avoid disputes is to notify the client in writing of a proposed transaction and then to get the client's informed consent in writing *before* making any distributions.[1] This detailed accounting or explanation of what is going to happen to the funds *before* settling a case and *before* accepting the funds for deposit should be done in writing. It would be preferable to get the client's written consent to every transaction, but this may not be practical. At the minimum, the lawyer should indicate that the transaction will occur unless the client contacts the lawyer.[2]

Clients can have a remarkable loss of memory—and can have second and third thoughts about the agreements they make with the lawyer or with the provider of the funds. Clients can have "settlers remorse"[3] after their friends and relatives tell them they settled for too much or too little. Clients can be emotionally involved in their cases to the point that they really don't want to settle at any price. Unsophisticated clients and even sophisticated clients often have the edge with respect to credibility in attorney-client disputes. The lawyer should protect both the firm and the client from subsequent disputes over who said what and alleged oral explanations.[4]

The lawyer should confirm by telephone, with third-party claimants, the balances claimed due the third parties from the funds before quoting settlement figures to the client. The lawyer should then confirm in writing, with the third parties, the amounts to be paid to the third parties from the settlement before allowing the client to accept the settlement.

## EXPLAINING THE DIFFERENCE BETWEEN GROSS AND NET SETTLEMENTS

When quoting settlement figures to a client, be careful to distinguish between gross amounts and net amounts to the client. Many bona fide disputes over fees arise out of the client not understanding what happens to the money after it reaches the trust account. The payment of fees, costs, and liens reduces the net amount they receive (or pay). The lawyer assumes the client was able to calculate the net amount to be paid or received before agreeing to a settlement. This is a dangerous assumption that leads to disputes and disciplinary complaints.

The lawyer should always give the client a written pro forma or proposed distribution accounting showing the difference between the gross settlement and the net settlement. The lawyer should only settle a case for a client after having documented in written notification to the client the gross and net amounts involved.

Periodic notification to a client of the firm advancing cost funds may eliminate the "surprise" element when it's time to reimburse costs and calculate fees.

The "Notice to Client of Proposed Settlement and Disbursement of Funds" included in Part VII demonstrates to the client the difference between net and gross amounts.

## NOTIFYING AND ACCOUNTING TO THE CLIENT

A lawyer has a duty to account to a client under ordinary fiduciary law and under disciplinary rules as well.[1] A prudent approach would be to notify a client immediately of any transaction affecting the balance of the trust account including funds in, funds out, and claims against the money. Some rules require "prompt" notification or "reasonable" notification.[2] Some rules may indicate specific time periods, such as monthly or quarterly or annually.

If a lawyer notifies the client immediately or concurrently, the lawyer should always be within permissible time requirements. What constitutes "prompt" notification is always a question of fact under the circumstances. In a perfect world, the client would be notified of the receipt of funds or disbursement of funds simultaneously with the event. In the real world, notification within a few days of the event would seem appropriate unless there were unusual circumstances.[3]

Accounting monthly as to trust account transactions and balances is the general norm unless there is some special reason for a shorter time period.[4] Notifying clients less frequently than monthly of trust account balances after transactions would probably be too long in most cases.[5]

The lawyer should read the local rules as to notification time periods and accounting time periods. Same-day notification of transactions and balances would probably always be a safe course of action.

## THE DUTY TO PAY THE CLIENT

The lawyer must pay the client all funds that belong to the client.[1] Normally, the lawyer must refund all unearned fees immediately upon being discharged by the client.[2] Whether the client needs the money back to hire another lawyer or has no reason or need for an immediate refund of the money is not a factor.[3] Immediate means immediate. This may result in disruption of the normal office routine to make a calculation of fees earned to the time of discharge to refund a proper balance. If there is any way the lawyer can refund the unearned money within twenty-four hours, he or she should do so to prevent an ethics complaint. Failure to refund unearned fees immediately after requested to do so is a common cause of ethics complaints.

Disputed fees need not be refunded immediately if the dispute is bona fide,[4] but the part of the unearned fees that is not in dispute must be refunded immediately.[5] The part in dispute should be resolved in accordance with the procedure used to resolve unpaid fee conflicts.[6]

For example, if a client were to have $5,000 remaining in the trust account, and the client simply wanted to drop the case and try to get the entire $5,000 refunded, the lawyer could hold on to the portion earned not billed and refund the nonearned portion. A disgruntled client might create a nonmeritorious dispute for an ulterior reason, such as trying to get the lawyer to reduce fees to avoid a nonmeritorious ethics complaint.

The general rule is that the lawyer must pay "promptly" all funds due to the client.[7] The lawyer may wait until he or she is satisfied that all deposits to the account have cleared and all required documents have been executed before making disbursements.[8] "Promptly" would be in accordance with what is reasonable under the circumstances and may not necessarily be "immediately."[9]

It would be wise to read the local rules to determine if there is a timing difference between refunding unearned fees and paying the client out of proceeds to be credited to the trust account. It would also be wise to determine if the determinative word is "immediately" or "promptly."

## THE COMMINGLING PROHIBITION

Do not forget that it is called a client's trust account, not a lawyer's trust account. Only client and third-party money is supposed to be in the account.[1]

The lawyer's money is not supposed to be in the account.[2] If the money clearly belongs to the lawyer, it is supposed to be removed immediately.[3] The IRS is especially unhappy about lawyers who allow their fees to remain in the trust account from one year into the next year.[4]

Remove your fee money as soon as it is earned and remove your cost reimbursement money as soon as it is available to you.[5] If there is a dispute over whether the fee is or is not earned and available to you, the money should be left in the account until the dispute is resolved, but should remain clearly labeled as such[6] (for example, Jones adv. Smith— Disputed Attorney's Fees).

If you have removed the fees and notified the client and the client objects to the fee, you must replace the fee money into the trust account until the dispute is resolved.[7]

At one time, it was customary for a lawyer to leave funds in the account to prevent service charges[8] or to cover any problems that might arise, but this is no longer permitted. The lawyer currently is allowed to keep a "nominal" or "reasonable" amount of money in the account to prevent bank charges or check-printing charges from eating into client money and to prevent bank charges when the amount of money in trust falls below the point where the bank waives all charges.[9]

While there is no uniformity or guarantee, about $200 of your money in the account at all times probably would not bother anyone. Check with IOLTA to determine what is permissible. Remember, IOLTA gets the interest on the money, so it is likely to be liberal in its estimate.

A lawyer may open a separate account called the "Client's Cost Account," from which the lawyer writes checks for client costs and to which the lawyer deposits the lawyer's money. Since it is not a client trust account, it would not be subject to the trust account prohibition on commingling, and the lawyer can keep as much of the lawyer's money as desired. The lawyer may deposit client reimbursements to this client's cost account, but not client advances, which would have to go to the trust account.

Paying personal expenses from the client trust account is a prohibited form of commingling even if the expenses are paid from fees that have been earned.[10] The lawyer should withdraw the earned fees from the trust account and deposit them to the office general account to record the fee income and thereafter draw the money out for transfer to a personal account to pay the personal expenses.[11] There is nothing unethical about paying personal expenses from the office account instead of from the personal account, but it is better management to pay personal expenses from a personal account.

Every year lawyers throughout America commit "aggressive stupidity" by using client trust account checks to pay bar dues, bar convention registrations, and CLE enrollment fees. These items routinely cause audits.

Some lawyers put their employees' withheld taxes and other deductions into the client trust account. This is not technically correct in most jurisdictions.[12] It is a *client's* trust account, not an *employees'* trust account. The lawyer can, if he or she wishes to, establish a separate account for taxes and deductions, but that must be different from the client trust account.

Some accountants erroneously combine the cash in the client trust account with the office and other cash in bank accounts, showing the balance as a payable or offset on the statement. It is probably prohibited commingling to combine client trust account cash with other cash on the statement or even to show it on the law firm's statements.

## NONCLIENT AND THIRD-PARTY CLAIMS

In some states, a lawyer's fiduciary and professional trust account funds responsibility is only to clients. In some states, a lawyer's duty with respect to trust account funds also runs to third parties and the lawyer can be disciplined for violating the fiduciary responsibility to the nonclient third party.[1]

Medical liens for medical services rendered are common examples of this type of third-party responsibility.[2] The California Medical Association has been known to pass out "do it yourself" disciplinary complaint forms to be filed against lawyers who settle cases without honoring medical liens. These complaints are investigated and prosecuted.

Disputes with non-client third parties. Third parties often have consensual[3] or statutory liens[4] on trust account funds. A client-patient often gives a lien to a doctor for medical services or to some other person for other reasons. Clients often obtain funds or credit against a claim or settlement. Once the lawyer acknowledges the lien of the third party, the lawyer may have a trust account fiduciary responsibility to the third party.[5] The lawyer can and will be disciplined under trust account rules if the lawyer violates the responsibility to the third party.[6] Clients may instruct a lawyer not to honor a lien, claiming that they will settle or pay the amount directly. The lawyer cannot accept these new instructions from the client without the acquiescence of the third party.[7]

A lawyer may not use the trust account to defeat the claims of third parties against a client by hiding client money from taxes, claims, creditors, their spouses, client's spouses, and so on.[8] A lawyer who uses the trust account to hide money for clients may have civil or criminal liability under fraudulent transfer laws or bankruptcy or insolvency laws.

In dealing with third parties and adversaries and nonclients, be careful to make clear from the first contact that you represent and are protecting the interest of only your client.[9] The third party may later claim that it was looking to you to protect its interests in the funds being collected or disbursed.

A form letter for disbursements to nonclients is included in Part VII.

## KNOW THE DIFFERENCES OF WHAT YOU ARE DEPOSITING INTO THE TRUST ACCOUNT

### Distinguishing Among Checks, Drafts, Collection Items, Cashier's Checks, Certified Checks, Money Orders, and Bank Money Orders

Most law schools no longer teach courses in bills and notes or negotiable instruments. Automated teller machines (ATMs) treat all "deposits" equally on a computer. Bank clerks and tellers are often unsophisticated and erroneously treat all checks and drafts the same.

Lawyers and others often do not understand that the nature of the instruments may determine when the funds are good and when disbursements may safely be made against the funds. There can be great differences between these instruments with serious civil and disciplinary consequences for the lawyer who does not understand the differences.

*Checks, drafts, and collection items.* The differences between checks, drafts, and collection items will vary from state to state. Normally checks will be presumed good and automatically accepted and honored a certain number of banking days after deposit. After that number of days has gone by, the lawyer can safely disburse funds against the check.

A draft or collection item (after a check has bounced once, it is normally treated as a collection item) is not "good funds" until the lawyer's bank has received credit or notification that the item has been paid or will be paid by the drawee bank. The lawyer, to be safe, should affirmatively confirm with his or her bank that the funds are good and can be disbursed against.

In some cases an insurance company will not honor its own settlement draft until it has compared signatures on the draft endorsement with signatures on the releases or other documents, or until certain documentations, such as dismissals, have been filed. This can take days or even weeks. (Read the section on the IOLTA snitch rule.)

*Cashier's checks vs. certified checks.* A certified check is almost like cash. It will be good except in the rarest of situations. A lawyer can normally feel safe disbursing against the certified check of a bank.

A cashier's check or teller's check or bank money order or other type of instrument is often nothing more than a common check written by a bank against itself. Payment can be stopped on these checks, and I have seen cases where banks have stopped payment on their cashier's checks at the request of depositors. A lawyer should not disburse against these checks until the statutory number of banking days has passed. This is a matter of state law and contract between the bank and the lawyer.

*Other items.* Money orders are just checks purchased from a private vendor such as a convenience store. These private vendors can and do go bankrupt leaving the checks unpaid. These money orders are nothing more than third-party checks even though they are fancy and look official.

Wire transfers and currency are not "instruments" but are the fastest and safest replacements for depositing instruments when immediate good funds are needed to allow safe disbursement of funds.

There may be state or federal laws allowing your bank to place a "hold" on funds for days or even weeks depending on the nature of the item "deposited" by the lawyer. These laws are sometimes euphemistically called "Expedited Funds Availability" laws.

Your bank may have contractual provisions allowing it to extend holding periods beyond the periods of federal or state laws. Your bank may be able to extend holding periods at its whim and discretion, causing your checks to bounce. The holding period might be affected by your state's IOLTA legislation. It is important that you talk to your banker and clearly understand your bank's "holding period" for each type of item you deposit.

## THE OFFENSE OF MISAPPROPRIATION

"Misappropriation" is a generic term sometimes used to describe failure to properly maintain a trust account even though the lawyer didn't "take" anything.[1] A disciplinary body may find misappropriation even though nothing was taken from a client or by a lawyer.[2] Misappropriation can include honest error or negligence in trust account maintenance[3] as well as including "taking" funds by the lawyer or using the funds of one client for the benefit of another client.[4]

Misappropriation can include intentionally or negligently creating a negative trust account balance (being out of trust) by issuing trust account checks before the related deposit is made or before the related funds are in fact collected and credited to the client trust account.[5]

Do not confuse the definition and use of the word "misappropriation" as used in connection with client trust accounts with the word "misappropriation" as used in some states for the crime of "misappropriation," which can be committed by obtaining funds for one purpose but using the funds for a different purpose.

## ENDORSING CLIENTS' NAMES ON CHECKS

Many lawyers build a limited power of attorney into the fee agreement empowering them to endorse the client's name and deposit the settlement or other checks made payable to the client or payable to both the lawyer and the client.[1] This procedure can prevent the client forging the lawyer's name on the check or forgetting to return the endorsed check or holding back on the endorsed check to try to negotiate a lower than agreed-on fee.

This procedure also lessens the likelihood of the check getting lost in transmission and return. This procedure also makes it possible for the clients to get their money sooner, since there won't be the delay of the mail going back and forth for signatures.

Some lawyers have the client come into the office to endorse the check in the office.

Generally it is permissible for the lawyer to obtain the power of attorney and to endorse and negotiate the check or draft,[2] but the lawyer should check if there is any local prohibition on this common practice.

### Signing Settlement Agreements

Although a limited power of attorney to endorse checks and drafts is normally permissible, this permission usually does not extend to signing settlement agreements for the client.[3] Even if allowed, it is a risky practice for the lawyer to sign the client's name to a settlement agreement, as the client may later claim the lawyer had no authority to sign a settlement or release for the client.

## CURRENCY TRANSACTIONS INVOLVING
## THE TRUST ACCOUNT

From time to time, a lawyer will be asked to deposit currency into a trust account or to pay out trust account funds with currency.

There is no reason to be paranoid when these requests are made, but you should be aware of some inherent problems and some possible reporting requirements.

It is common English to use the words "cash" and "currency" interchangeably, but there is a difference for various reporting laws. Currency is the money in circulation. Coins and paper money such as one-dollar bills and one-hundred-dollar bills are properly referred to as currency. "Cash" is often defined by various reporting laws to include "monetary instruments," including cashier's checks, treasurer's checks, traveler's checks, money orders, and bank checks. The definitions are more clouded because some laws require reporting when the amount exceeds $10,000 (typically currency) and some laws require reporting when an individual item amount is less than $10,000, but when the cumulative total of each item less than $10,000 exceeds $10,000 in the aggregate.[1] For example, a $5,000 transaction and $4,000 transaction might not require reporting, but when a $3,000 transaction is added to the $9,000, then all three transactions must be reported. This is a very complicated subject.

People often have a valid reason for dealing in currency instead of checks. The recipient may need cash for the legitimate needs of a business. There are many industries where it is normal and regular to deal in currency at wholesale and at retail. The recipient may be going to a place in or out of the country where a trust account check or a bank check may not be easily negotiable and the recipient prefers to deal with currency, or currency may get a higher rate of foreign exchange than traveler's checks or bank checks.

People may have perfectly valid sources of currency for deposit to the trust account. They may be bringing in money from a foreign country with difficult foreign exchange rules. They may be bringing you funds from their cash savings hoard under the mattress or from someone else's cash savings hoard. They may have won large sums of money gambling at a local casino. There are people who do not believe in banks and keep everything in currency.

### Important Issues When Dealing with Cash

Be aware of the following problems in dealing with cash:

1. Safeguard the currency.[2] You are responsible for safeguarding the currency. In former times, every law office had a safe to temporarily store valuable papers and items. Very few offices have safes anymore. One must be careful in transporting the cash to and from the bank. If you are in possession of a large amount of cash or expect to be, ask your insurance agent if the property or cash of third parties is insured under your policy, and what it would cost to get a rider to insure the cash both on and off the premises and while enroute to or from the bank. You may wish to bring the currency to the bank in installments to protect the cash from possible robbery.

2. Make a preliminary investigation. Ask the client the source of cash being deposited. Ask the client why the funds are in cash instead of check or wire transfer. You don't want to find yourself being indicted as a coconspirator in a bank robbery or for money laundering. Exercise an appropriate amount of "due diligence."

3. Be extremely careful if any of the money is going to or for a politician either in or out of the United States. There are severe penalties for illegal campaign contributions under federal, state, and local laws, including possible criminal violations. There are also federal laws concerning bribes and overseas Foreign Corrupt Practices as defined by various laws. The client may later claim that you knew all along what the funds would be used for and that you told the client it was perfectly legal.

4. Be careful if you are rendering few or nominal legal services other than to process the currency. If the client simply wants to use you as a bank, tell the client to go to a bank.

5. Be aware of federal cash transaction reporting rules.[3] Your banker can probably give you a three-minute course in reporting cash transactions. There are federal reporting requirements if the amount of cash is $10,000 or more in a single transaction or in a series of transactions. These requirements give the customs and narcotics people the right to seize cash that has not been properly reported or that might be the fruits of a crime. These laws also create a punishable offense for not telling the government everything it might be interested in.

6. Government authorities may cause a firm to spend a lot of time and possibly money trying to get the names of clients and other

information when there has been a cash transaction. A law firm has an ethical and a legal obligation to protect client confidences. The government authorities will want to ignore these "technicalities" and try to convince the firm that resisting the government is fruitless, claiming it will win any court battles against the firm. A lawyer, unfortunately, will have to advise them that the firm is not free to voluntarily release client information without the client's consent.

You should ask the client on receiving the currency or paying the currency if the client will waive attorney-client privilege for government investigations and process. If the client refuses to waive confidentiality, be sure the legal fee represents an anticipated fight with the IRS.

There is an excellent article on this subject, "Disclosure of Currency Transaction Violations: When, How, and What If You Don't?," by Mark F. Sommer, published in the ABA periodical *Tax Lawyer* 47, no. 1. The law in this area is changing daily, and your banker is a good source of current information.

Also, see this book's section on "Ethical Problems Caused by Service of Process," as well as the form letter "Notice to Client Concerning Service of Process" in Part VII.

7. Be aware of state or local cash reporting rules. There are often state and local rules concerning both the receipt and payment of cash. Often these rules are intended to prevent elderly people from being swindled or to alert police to the possibility of cash being withdrawn to pay kidnap ransom, or the like. Here again, a banker can probably give you a quick course in current law.

8. Get Social Security numbers and descriptions. Depending on the state of the law and the law involved, the law firm may be required to get Social Security numbers (also called Taxpayer Employer Identification Numbers) from the person to whom the cash is given or from the person from whom you receive cash. An attempt should be made to get these numbers even if unsuccessful.

9. Dealing with foreigners. A lawyer or client may have additional reporting responsibilities and possibly income tax withholding responsibilities when the currency is going into or out of the country.

Lastly, when dealing with currency, advise the client that the client may or may not have reporting requirements and that the client has not engaged you to give a legal opinion on the subject and that you do not accept professional responsibility for advising on compliance with currency reporting laws.

## WITHHELD PAYROLL TAXES

Employees are not clients. Withheld taxes are treated as trust funds under federal tax laws. Some bar prosecutorial authorities treat failure to account for or to report or pay withheld employee taxes the same as failure to account for or to report or pay client trust funds.[1]

Treat withheld employee taxes with the same care as client funds.[2] Do not, however, put withheld employee taxes in the client trust account.[3] The client trust account is for client money, not for payroll taxes.

Consider opening an employee tax trust account in addition to the client trust account.

Many firms maintain a separate payroll bank account. The firm deposits the gross payroll into the account and pays the net payroll to the employees, leaving the withheld taxes in the account until the withheld taxes are deposited or paid to the appropriate government agency.

# PART IV

---

## DEALING WITH SPECIAL
## TRUST ACCOUNT PROBLEMS

## AVOID EXTREMELY COMPLEX
## COMMERCIAL TRANSACTIONS

Most lawyers are not equipped economically to handle major complex commercial business transactions. These complex transactions should be left to banks and escrow companies, which make a business out of publishing the appropriate notices, making the appropriate filings, getting the appropriate clearances and releases, and deciding disputed claims to funds. Various government agencies may be required by law to receive notices. Failure to provide these notices can result in civil or criminal liability to the client and the lawyer. The lawyer can and should review and be responsible for preparing and reviewing the instructions, the contracts, and the like, but should be wary about accepting the responsibility for doing things at which the lawyer is not competent and that may or may not be covered by malpractice insurance.

There may be a serious question as to the conscionability of a law firm charging legal fees to do this clerical work. I have seen large law firms charge clients partner rates to do things in a business transaction that should have been done by bank clerks at a tiny fraction of the firm's fee. If, however, the client is aware of the alternatives and is still willing to pay the law firm to do the work, then I don't see a problem.

## BEWARE OF EXOTIC DEALINGS
## YOU DON'T UNDERSTAND

Frauds and con artists often swindle lawyers and their clients, both sophisticated and unsophisticated, using meaningless gobbledygook double-talk. They depend on the use of a lawyer's trust account to give an air of legitimacy to the transaction. They know that many people will depend on the lawyer to be sure the deal is honest.

A lawyer is sometimes embarrassed to admit he or she doesn't understand a transaction and allows the client to persuade him or her to issue trust account checks against funds that never existed to begin with.

You, as the lawyer, may find yourself with both an ethical and legal responsibility to make good the losses of your clients or third parties who are defrauded.

Be very cautious and even suspicious when foreign trust companies or banks and double escrows, weird letters of credit, and wire transfers are involved. Don't be embarrassed or ashamed to ask your bank manager if he or she understands what is going on and whether it is legitimate. You have a degree in law, not in banking. Don't be ashamed to admit you don't understand the transaction.

Avoid bad-smelling transactions. When someone wants to use your trust account for something that just doesn't smell right, be careful. You have a law firm, not a bank. Clients often want to use lawyer's trust accounts for money laundering, illegal campaign contributions, bribes, avoiding various reports, and a host of other illegal acts. Investigate carefully when a client wants you to accept or pay cash or wire transfers to or from exotic locations. There are often bona fide, perfectly legitimate reasons for using a trust account for unusual transactions, but be careful. There are often very valid reasons for not disclosing the identity of a client or the source or distributions of funds. On the other hand, the transactions may be questioned years later and the client may be long gone, leaving you to face disciplinary or criminal proceedings.

## ETHICAL PROBLEMS CAUSED BY SERVICE OF PROCESS

Note: This chapter deals with service of process to get trust account information by other than a bar disciplinary agency.

In most, if not all, jurisdictions, the attorney-client privilege or other privileges cannot be asserted in a disciplinary proceeding or investigation, normally on the theory that the information is just as confidential in the possession of the disciplinary authorities as it would be with the lawyer.[1]

In some jurisdictions, the disciplinary authorities may issue secret subpoenas and obtain trust account information without notifying the lawyer until long after the records have been delivered to the bar disciplinary authorities.

Service of process to get information from the trust account or to get access to the trust account raises ethical issues that are not covered by the trust account rules but that may or may not be covered by other ethics rules (client confidences, work product, etc.).

The process served or the information sought might relate to a specific client or group of clients or to the lawyer or the lawyer's firm. Typical process would be a subpoena duces tecum or other discovery in a civil or criminal suit or a summons in an IRS investigation.

A lawyer has an absolute duty to protect all privileges, secrets, and confidences of a client and to assert them on the client's behalf unless expressly instructed to waive the privileges by the client.[2] Typical privileges that must be raised by the lawyer if appropriate include the attorney-client privilege, the privilege against self-incrimination, and the privilege against unreasonable search and seizure, as well as various privacy act confidences under various state laws.

The lawyer should normally, as a first step, communicate with the client or clients whose confidences will be affected to determine whether they wish to waive privileges. Absent an informed waiver, the lawyer must assert the privileges.[3]

There are at least two schools of thought on what you should do when served with process or the threat of service of process.

1. Give them what they want. Why spend the firm's time and money or the client's time and money protecting client confidences if the subpoenaing authority can probably get the

same information from banks or third parties or if the subpoenaing authority could probably prevail in a court proceeding?

2. The lawyer's duty to the client is absolute. A lawyer is obligated to do everything appropriate to protect the client confidences of all clients, not just the one about whom information is sought. If parties seeking trust account information claim they can get the same information from third parties, let them do so. If parties seeking trust account information claim they can get the same information from the bank, let them do so. They can do their job, which is to seek information from the trust account, and you can do your job, which is to protect the client confidences of all clients.

Two related sample form letters are included in Part VII. One is for clients (Form 7) and the other is for the person or agency seeking information (Form 8). The law in this area is in a constant state of flux and you should ask the appropriate ethics agency for suggestions as to the proper course of conduct.

## THE DISHONORED TRUST ACCOUNT DEPOSIT TRAP

A bounced or dishonored deposit to a trust account can be a trap for the negligent.[1] A lawyer should not write checks against deposits until the deposit has cleared and good funds are available in the trust account.[2]

If a lawyer has written checks to the firm, to third parties, or to clients, the lawyer may have serious disciplinary problems if the deposited check bounces.

If the lawyer wrote the checks before the deposited funds were properly credited to the account, the lawyer was technically out of trust the moment the checks were written because the checks were issued against nonexistent funds. A computerized reconstruction of the lawyer's trust account would show the account to be out of trust. If the lawyer held the checks until the deposit was credited to the account, the lawyer would have to prove to the disciplinary investigators that the checks were not sent.

If the deposit check bounces and the checks the lawyer wrote clear, then the lawyer may have used other clients' funds in the account to make good on checks having nothing to do with those other clients. Accordingly, the lawyer will have compounded the problem. Even if the deposited item clears on collection at a later date or even if the lawyer makes good the checks written out of the lawyer's personal funds, the lawyer is still at fault.

On audit the lawyer could be in trouble in either situation.

It is important to remember that "fault" is not in issue. The reason the deposit check bounced may mitigate the lawyer's disciplinary punishment, if any, but the offense has occurred.

It is clearly the more prudent course for the lawyer to wait until the deposit is good funds in the account and then issue the checks at that point.

## HANDLING "RUSH-RUSH" SETTLEMENTS

From time to time a client may pressure a lawyer to expedite payment of funds to the client from the trust account. In some cases, the only reason the client settled the case was to get to urgently needed funds.

The lawyer who issues a check to a client against a check or draft that has not cleared is at great risk if the deposited item bounces, for the lawyer will have used the funds of other clients to honor the check that should have not been written.[1]

Even if the check does clear and everything turns out all right, the lawyer is still at risk of disciplinary action for having been technically out of trust until the deposited item became irreversibly good.

You should consider the following solutions if you face this problem:

1. Have the other side pay in currency.

2. Have the other side pay with a certified check (not a cashier's check, which is very different because payment can be stopped on a cashier's check).

3. Open a trust account at the same branch of the same bank on which the check is written. The interbank credit and debit will be instantaneous without waiting for the clearinghouse.

4. Have the funds wired to your trust account. Upon receipt of the wire, the funds are good. Have the person wiring the funds indicate who at your bank to notify of the sending of the funds. You should alert that person to notify you by telephone of the receipt so you can disburse against the wired funds. Be sure to create appropriate paper or hard-copy records for audit purposes.

5. When the bank is out of town, ask your bank to messenger the check to the other bank with instructions to "wire fate." Wire fate is a banking term whereby the drawee bank wires to the depositing bank the fate of the inquiry, i.e., "The check is good and funds are being sent" or "The check is not good." Upon receipt of the wire, the funds are good.

6. If permitted under local rules, you can make a personal loan of personal funds against the trust account funds. You may be required to go through several formal steps, including obtaining a formal promissory note from the client and instructions to repay the

note from the trust funds. This is absolutely forbidden in some jurisdictions.

7. Some states have special rules for real estate or commercial situations where the lawyer's trust account is being used as an escrow account.

## GETTING THE FEE AS QUICKLY AS POSSIBLE

A lawyer may be tempted to violate the conditions of deposit of a draft or check to get the fee as soon as possible. It is not uncommon for a lawyer to receive both a settlement agreement or general release and a settlement check at the same time with instructions that the check may be endorsed and deposited after the settlement agreement or general release has been signed by the client.

The lawyer may want to sign the client's name to both the release or settlement agreement and to the settlement draft. If the lawyer has an express written grant of a power of attorney in the fee agreement or other agreement to sign settlements and negotiable instruments, then the lawyer may sign both, clearly indicating he or she is signing the client's name under the power of attorney.[1]

A written agreement is crucial because a client may forget an oral delegation of the right to sign a settlement agreement, and unhappy clients with poor memories often file both disciplinary and forgery complaints.[2]

Endorsing a client's name to a settlement draft or check pursuant to powers given in a fee agreement is a common practice where permitted. However, signing a client's name to a settlement agreement or general release can be risky for the lawyer, even under a power of attorney to do so.[3]

## OUT OF TRUST = IN TROUBLE

It is important to understand the meaning of the words "out of trust."

"Out of trust" means that the liability of the lawyer or firm to clients and others from monies received is greater than the cash balances available in the trust account to pay all the liabilities.[1] One could say that the trust account was insolvent in that if the trust account had to be liquidated on the spot, there would not be enough cash in the account to pay all the liabilities.

It is possible to be out of trust with respect to a specific client or matter. It is also possible to be out of trust as to all matters combined. For example, if the bookkeeper embezzled a large sum of money from the trust account, the entire account would be out of trust.[2] If a deposit of trust account money was erroneously credited to client A instead of client B, the total trust account would be in balance, but client B's account would be out of trust and client A's account would be out of balance.

It is also possible to be out of trust on a given day due to a delay in crediting a deposit to an account or a delay in the clearing of a check.

It is also possible to be out of trust due to an honest error by the lawyer or due to a bank mistake.[3]

Being "out of trust" is a mathematical calculation. Once it is determined that the lawyer is, or has been, out of trust, an investigation by a disciplinary investigator may begin or become more serious.

## USING A BACKUP LINE OF CREDIT

In some states, lawyers can negotiate with their bank to provide a backup line of credit or overdraft privileges for the lawyer on the trust account. With this line or overdraft privileges, the lawyer can write checks that would be covered and honored, even though there is not enough money in the client trust account to pay the check presented.

Depending on the IOLTA rules in the lawyer's state, the bank would only have to notify IOLTA if a check in fact bounces. In basketball, it would be called a "no harm, no foul" rule. In those states, the only concern of the IOLTA and bar disciplinary authorities is to get maximum interest income for IOLTA and to protect the monies of the clients. Since the client got his or her money and IOLTA got its interest, no one was in fact hurt; and no one will care or report a check that was not good when presented. Alternatively, since no one was hurt, there may not be an investigation.

In other states, the mere presentment of an overdraft requires notification to IOLTA and the state bar, even if the check is made good without being bounced.[1]

One of the consequences of notification could be an automatic audit of the attorney's trust account for a three-year period, which might or might not turn up deficiencies that were long ago corrected.

Having a backup line of credit for a client trust account or having overdraft privileges for the client trust account might save you a lot of wasted time and money.

In most states, the mere presentment of a check that was not adequately covered by the balance in the trust account would be automatic "misappropriation" and grounds for a complaint and an investigation.[2]

You should check with local IOLTA and disciplinary authorities whether a backup line of credit will prevent investigations.

# PART V

---

# KEEPING TRUST ACCOUNT RECORDS

## SEGREGATE AND DISTINGUISH CLIENT TRUST ACCOUNT RECORDS AND CHECKS FROM OTHER RECORDS AND CHECKS

It is good practice to segregate client trust account records and cancelled checks from other records and checks. Maintain and store them separate and apart from the regular office or personal checks and records. Some states require this physical segregation of trust account records, but it is good practice whether or not required.

In most states a law firm must be able to produce the trust account cancelled checks and records on proper demand,[1] and it will not do any good to claim time is needed to find the trust account records because they are, or were, commingled with the regular banking records. The period of time for record retention for trust account banking records may be different from the period of time for retention or destruction of other client or banking records.[2]

Do everything possible to prevent accidental commingling of trust account records and checks with non-trust account records and checks. Try to keep the trust account records and cancelled checks and endorsement stamps and other supplies in a different drawer or cabinet than other records. Try to mark them with distinguishing marks (for example, red labels or folders) to prevent accidental confusion of trust account supplies and implements and non-trust account supplies and implements.

Use a red checkbook for the trust account and a green checkbook for the general office account (red for danger and green for profit).

Have the bank print different-colored checks and deposit tickets and even different-sized checks for the client trust account.

A very conservative approach that I have never seen in practice would be to use a different institution for trust accounts. I have only seen this done where the amounts exceeded the insurance required.

## TYPICAL RECORDS REQUIREMENTS

This section essentially repeats another section in Part I to provide an example of the kinds of records statutorily required to be kept in connection with trust accounts.

Other records, which may or may not be statutorily required, are described in the next section.

Various state bar authorities and IOLTA authorities require records to be kept in a certain way and to include certain information. Unfortunately, there is no uniformity from state to state as to the requirements or the vocabulary used to describe what is wanted.

The problem is further complicated by the fact that there is not necessarily any connection between generally accepted accounting practices and what is required. The vocabulary used to describe what is required may bear no relation to the vocabulary used in the world of business or the world of accounting.

The rules promulgated by the Board of Governors of the State Bar of California are included here as a typical set of state rules and as a general reference point to the vocabulary used and the types of records and reports one state demands. Do not assume that these rules will apply in whole or in part anywhere else. It is imperative that local rules containing local vocabulary and local requirements be obtained and studied.

> A member shall, from date of receipt of client funds through the period ending five years from the date of appropriate disbursement of such funds, maintain:
>
> (a) A written ledger for each client on whose behalf funds are held that sets forth
>
> (i) the name of such client,
>
> (ii) the date, amount, and source of all funds received on behalf of such client,
>
> (iii) the date, amount, payee, and purpose of each disbursement made on behalf of such client, and
>
> (iv) the current balance for such client.
>
> (b) A written journal for each bank account that sets forth
>
> (i) the name of such account,

(ii) the date, amount, and client affected by each debit and credit, and

(iii) the current balance in such account;

(c) all bank statements and cancelled checks for each bank account; and

(d) each monthly reconciliation (balancing) of (a), (b), and (c).

## COMMON TRUST ACCOUNT RECORDS AND DOCUMENTS

Original documents that should be kept segregated and available[1] include the following:

1. Cancelled trust account checks
2. Deposit tickets or copies of deposit tickets showing which items have been deposited to the trust account on which dates (and, although not required, it is good practice that all items deposited to the client trust account be photocopied before deposit, including the backs to show endorsements or lack of endorsements)
3. Bank notices of items submitted for collection rather than deposit (typically checks that have bounced and certain types of drafts)
4. Bank notices of wire transfers in and wire transfers out
5. Bank statements
6. Bank reconciliations
7. Checkbooks
8. Check stubs
9. Vouchers
10. Ledgers
11. Schedules used to adjust bank or book balances
12. Documents that should be obtainable from closed files as needed:

   a. Fee agreements showing how fees and costs are calculated and how money is or is not supposed to go through the trust account
   b. Copies of notices to clients of deposits to the account and new account balances
   c. Copies of notices to clients of disbursements against the account and the new account balances
   d. Calculations used to determine amounts of withdrawals from the account
   e. Copies of lien agreements or assignments to third parties
   f. Copies of bills paid from the trust account
   g. The client file

## "Records" Required by Various Bar Acts

*A "ledger" for each client (single or multiple matters).* In accounting language this would be called the subsidiary ledger because each page (it could run more than one page) represents one client or one matter.[2] This could also be called the detail ledger because it provides the details for a single account.

Note that a separate ledger is required for each client, not for each matter. Accordingly, a lawyer would have one ledger account for the Smith real estate closing and another ledger account for the Jones estate and another ledger account for the Aconite sale of real estate matter. A lawyer is only required to have one ledger account for the Ketchum collection agency, although there may be hundreds of different collection matters included in the single Ketchum ledger account. A firm certainly could maintain a separate ledger account for each Ketchum collection matter, and indeed it might be less complicated to do so, but the firm is not required to do so.

Normally, the client ledger accounts must contain the following information on a current running basis, preferably after each transaction but at least once a month:

- The name of the client
- The specific matter if the client has more than one ledger account
- The dates, amounts, descriptions, and sources of all amounts received for or from that client as shown on that ledger account
- The dates, amounts, payees, and purposes of each payee for each disbursement
- The current running balance preferably updated and computed after each transaction, but at least monthly for that ledger account

*Schedule of client balances (total of all client ledger balances).* In accountants' language, this "schedule" would be called the control account because the dollar total of all the individual client ledger accounts should add up to be the same as the total dollar balances of the schedules of client balances.

*Cash receipts journal for each bank trust account.* Entries should be made to the journal on a daily basis showing deposits to the trust account the day the money is received ready for deposit.

This is not much different from any receipt transaction, except that it is not going into the ordinary check register but rather a special cash receipts journal. In most cases the simple checking account running balance format that comes with your printed bank checks would be adequate to meet this requirement, but a separate journal repeating the same information into a special book called a cash receipts journal may be necessary under local rules.

*Cash disbursements journal for each bank trust account.*

*Monthly bank reconciliation.* Three-way reconciliation of cash in bank per bank statement to total balance of all client accounts (control) to the totals of individual client accounts (detail also called the ledger).

*Written records vs. computer records.* The rules in many states require the various trust account records to be "written" or "in writing."[3] Most states require a monthly or transactional printout of the required schedules and information. In some states it is possible for the records to exist only on a disk or tape, with a printout being made when required. The rules are not consistent from state to state.

Lawyers and firms wishing to keep trust account records on computer would be wise to prepare hard-copy printouts at least monthly. The hard copy will be invaluable in the event of a computer crash, which would wipe out unbacked-up data. The hard copy will also be invaluable if the data could no longer be read because of a vendor discontinuing equipment or discontinuing support of either software or hardware, rendering the memory unreadable.

It is not possible to recommend any specific software, since most trust account software is a component part of a larger billing package and all programs depend on the lawyer's level of computer skills.

# SPECIAL TRUST ACCOUNT TERMS

## The Journal (Also Called the Account Journal)

The word "journal" as used in client trust accounting has very little if anything to do with the word "journal" as used in generally accepted accounting principles or the accounting records normally found in any enterprise other than a law office.[1]

The terms "journal," "account journal," and "client balances" are statutorily created terms and must be defined by the local rules and the IOLTA rules.

By whatever name or names locally used, the journal is usually a list of all of the client trust account balances kept in a particular bank trust account as of a given date with a grand total of all of the client trust account balances which should equal (be reconciled to) to the reconciled bank balance.

This schedule should be prepared and reviewed monthly, with hard copies kept for audit by the disciplinary authorities.

If the lawyer had only one client trust account bank account, the total of all the individual client trust account balances (sometimes called the ledger cards) should equal the reconciled bank balance of cash in the account.

Try not to be confused by the terms "debit" or "credit," which are often loosely and confusingly used in some trust account rules. A "debit" is an increase in cash in the bank trust account with an equal "credit" or increase in the balances of the individual clients' accounts. A "credit" is a check or withdrawal from the bank account with an equal "debit" or reduction in the balances of the individual clients' trust accounts.

The account journal, by whatever name, normally should contain the following information:

1. The name and address of the bank location where the account is kept
2. The account number of the bank account
3. The amount and date and source of each deposit or credit to the account
4. The amount and date and number and payee of each check written against the account.

5. The client affected by the addition or reduction in the account

6. The current balance of the account

If the local rules don't require all of the above information on a single report, it is still a good practice to have the above schedule of information readily available with the trust account data for presentation or immediate reconstruction when necessary.

## The Bank Reconciliation

The term "bank reconciliation" is an ordinary commercial term. You should be familiar with it from your personal checking account. It has the same meaning in general accounting and in trust accounting. This is a reconciliation of the balance as shown on the statement received from the bank to the balance of the cash in the bank account as shown on your books. (It may have other names in your jurisdiction.)

Normal items to be considered in the reconciliation include outstanding checks and deposits in transit. (You've mailed them in, but they're not shown by the bank.) Bank service charges or interest not yet entered on your books must also be taken into account in the reconciliation. Almost every commercial bank will provide you with the mechanical format to be followed. It is often on the back of the statement you receive in the mail. Most commercial computer bookkeeping systems, such as Quicken, contain a bank reconciliation module.

Most banks send bank statements with cancelled checks on a monthly basis. If you insist, the bank can cut off the statement as of any day of the month or while you wait if there is an urgency. Banks won't want to do it, because you're upsetting their routine, but they can do it.

## The Ledger

The word "ledger" as used in trust account definitions may bear absolutely no similarity to the word "ledger" as used in general accounting. In trust account accounting records, the ledger is often the card or record showing all income and expenses and the running balance of a particular client's balance in the trust account. It is really a form of accounts payable detail in accounting language.[2]

You must keep the bank reconciliations, journals, and ledgers for examination along with the other trust account books and records.[3]

## Double and Triple Reconciliations

The terms "reconciliation," "double reconciliation," and "triple reconciliation" are sometimes found in the various rules. The terms may have different meanings in different states. The terms as used here are generic and are approximately correct in most or all states.

*Trust accounts reconciliation.* A trust accounts reconciliation is a reconciliation of the grand total of all trust accounts (the general ledger account balance) to the individual totals of all the trust accounts. In accounting terminology this is sometimes called reconciling the detail to the control.

The individual client record may be called other names in your jurisdiction. You have to reconcile the individual trust account balances to the grand total of all trust account balances.[4] The process in accounting terms as indicated is reconciling the control to the detail.

*Double reconciliation.* The reconciliation of the detail to the control is one reconciliation. The reconciliation of the bank statement to the books is another reconciliation. These two reconciliations must reconcile to each other (and the world will be a happy place for all concerned) in most jurisdictions.

*Triple reconciliation.* Some jurisdictions require a monthly triple reconciliation of the following:

1. The cash per client trust account bank statement must be reconciled at least monthly to the trust account cash in bank balance per books.
2. Individual client trust account balances per "ledger cards" must be reconciled at least monthly to the balance of the client trust accounts per "journal."
3. The balance per books of client trust account cash in bank must also be reconciled monthly to the balance per "journal" of client trust accounts.

## COMPUTER RECORDS VS. HANDWRITTEN RECORDS

(Note: I wish to acknowledge the assistance of Ken Alwin, Esq., of Mutual Software, a management consulting firm in Minneapolis, for his assistance in providing information current as of early 1996. Ken and I both caution lawyers that technology changes and new products come into the marketplace daily. Any reference to software or systems should be considered areas to look into rather than recommendations.)

I recommend that a new lawyer or any lawyer who has not previously been in private practice or who has never dealt with client funds or third-party funds keep handwritten trust account records until the lawyer truly understands the flow of money into and out of the account and understands the various records, reconciliations, etc., required by the rules.

When the volume of checks or transactions becomes burdensome, computer-generated checks and records can be used. Under no circumstances, however, should a computer or other mechanical device or other person, no matter how trusted, ever sign a trust account check.

What a lawyer or firm eventually does or doesn't do will reflect their technical ability to understand and run the system. Additionally, vendor support available and needed should be considered as well as the amount of money the lawyer is willing or able to spend. The needs of a firm's particular practice is of course paramount. A tax or corporate practice that handles client money once a month has very different needs than a high-volume personal injury, real estate, or collection practice.

Most accounting and billing software packages have a trust account component or module. Most check-writing and general accounting software packages also have a trust account component or can be adapted to be used for a trust account. One would not ordinarily spend the amount of money involved to buy a complete accounting package just to get a trust account component.

There are some dedicated single-purpose trust account software programs available. Some of the single-purpose packages available are state-specific or practice-specific and some are generic.

## Choosing a Software Program

It is difficult if not impossible to recommend specific software. New programs and upgrades quickly make existing state-of-the-art programs obsolete. Reviewing a local bar journal or local legal newspaper is one way to find out what is available where the lawyer is going to practice. Appendix A, "Where to Get Help," contains sources to call to get assistance on what is currently available and worthwhile to the particular lawyer or firm. A few integrated systems that include a trust account module are Advantage, Time & Management System, Juris, ProLaw, Elite, and PC Law, Jr. Alternatively, one could adapt Quicken for trust account maintenance, as demonstrated in the next section. A telephone call to a local bar-employed law office management practice advisor or a CPA is usually worth the time.

At the minimum, the lawyer should always sign trust account checks by hand after being satisfied the checks are proper and are being written against good funds. The rules don't require a handwritten "wet ink" original signature on trust account checks, but it is good practice. The lawyer should also personally review the reconciliations to be sure the trust accounts are in balance and appear normal.

If no state- or practice-specific programs are available, the lawyer may want to create an appropriate spreadsheet that complies with the local rules.

Almost all rules require monthly or more frequent hard-copy printouts of trust account records, reports, and reconciliations, to eliminate the defense of "computer crash" should there be no records to audit. Publishers of software and manufacturers of hardware often go out of business or no longer support their products, making the memory unreadable by modern equipment or programs.

## USING QUICKEN® TO RECORD ACCOUNT TRANSACTIONS AND PRINT REPORTS

(Note: My thanks to Mike Winkler, CPA, of Kelson, Rood, Stoll & Winkler, CPA's of Los Angeles, California, for helping to write this chapter. He prepared this "no brainer, connect the dots" list at my request for those who want to use Quicken for general bookkeeping and trust accounts bookkeeping and reports.)

Quicken is easily the most common bookkeeping software package used by small law firms. It is not an entire accounting system.

Quicken can be used to do the bookkeeping for trust accounts. It can also be used for writing trust account deposits and checks, but I recommend it primarily as a way of recording handwritten checks and deposits. Here is a runthrough of the procedure.

*Recording Client Trust Account Transactions on Quicken 7.0 for DOS*

*Opening Up a New Trust Account*
1. From the main menu select "Select Account."
2. Select "New Account."
3. Select "Bank Account."
4. Enter "Trust Account" for name.
5. Record the opening balance and date, if any.
6. Record the bank account number under "Description (Optional)."

*Entering Transactions for Deposits into a Trust Account*
1. From the main menu select "Select Account."
2. Select "Trust Account."
3. Enter date in the "date" field.
4. Enter "Dep" in the "number" field.
5. Enter "Deposit" in the "payee" field.
6. Enter the dollar amount in the "deposit" field.
7. Enter "Funds Received" in the "memo" field.
8. If a new client, enter "Trust Acct." in the "category" field.
9. Select "add to category list."
10. Select "I" for income account and hit "enter" three times.
11. Hit "CTRL" and "C" to choose the category.
12. Hit "CTRL" and "INS" to set up client name.

13. Enter client name (Last name first) in the "name" field.
14. Select "S" in "Income, Expense or Subcategory" field.
15. You can bypass the next three questions by pressing "enter" until "OK to Record Transaction" appears.
16. Enter "Record Transaction."

*Entering Transactions for Payment from a Trust Account*
1. Enter the date in the "date" field.
2. Enter the check number in the "number" field.
3. Enter the payee in the "payee" field.
4. Enter the amount in the "payment" field.
5. Enter description in the "memo" field.
6. Hit "CTRL" and "C" to select client. Highlight desired client from Category List.
7. Hit "enter" three times to accept client and "record transaction."

*Creating a Report*
1. Select "Create Reports" from the main menu.
2. Select "Personal Reports," or "Home Reports."
3. Select "Itemized Categories."
4. Enter "Clients' Trust Account Report" as the title.
5. Select "Custom Date."
6. Enter F9 "Filter."
7. Cursor down to "Selecting Categories to include," enter "Y," and keep hitting "enter" until the list of categories appears. To include in the report the trust category and all subcategories, which represent clients, hit the "spacebar" next to the category name. Hit "enter" when all clients have been selected.
8. Enter desired date.
9. Hit "Enter" and the report will be generated.

# PART VI

## THE TEN COMMANDMENTS OF GOOD TRUST ACCOUNTS

## TEN RULES OF GOOD TRUST ACCOUNT PROCEDURES

These ten rules are generic. They will apply anywhere in the United States. It is also important to know your local rules and where to get help locally. Get a copy of your local trust account rules. Learn the telephone number of the ethics hot line maintained by your state and local bar associations. Learn the name and phone number of the chair of the bar association ethics committee. Don't be afraid to call as many people as you can when you have a trust account question. There are no foolish or stupid questions when it comes to trust accounts.

If you follow the general rules set forth in this section, you'll go a long way toward staying out of trouble.

### Rule 1
### Have a trust account.

You can't properly use what you don't have. Be sure it is clearly identified as "Client Trust Account" or use some other language that makes it clear that the account is a trust account. At the very least, you should have a checking client trust account, a client trust safe deposit box, and, when appropriate, a savings client trust account. You should have these even though you have no immediate need for them. When you do need them, you'll be ready to go. The account should be in a federally insured institution within the geographic boundaries of your state.

### Rule 2
### Never let anyone else sign your trust account.

Never allow another person to sign trust account checks. Do not use mechanical or rubberstamp signatures. Do not allow your bookkeeper or secretary or paralegal or spouse to sign on the account. If the trusted secretary or bookkeeper of many years opts for early retirement down in Brazil some Friday afternoon using the latest trust account deposit as the funding for retirement, you will have civil and disciplinary responsibility, including possible loss of license if you don't cover the defalcation. An intervening defalcation won't relieve you of responsibility.

## Rule 3
## Obtain and understand your IOLTA
## (Interest On Lawyers' Trust Account) rules.

Every state requires that lawyers put trust account funds into special accounts where the interest on the account goes to fund some activity such as legal aid or a client trust account protection fund. Your state will have such a mandatory system, your bank will have an agreement with the bar organization, and you will have no option but to use the IOLTA account in most situations. Most IOLTA banks are obligated to notify the bar disciplinary authorities if one of your checks is presented against insufficient funds, even if it doesn't bounce. The bar may send out auditors to investigate your trust account. They may investigate your account for many years, looking for mistakes. They might not limit their investigation to the single transaction that caused the bank to notify the disciplinary authorities.

If the amount of interest is likely to be significant because of the amount of money or the length of time, you should not use an IOLTA account, but rather you should open another special trust account for that one client, giving the interest to the client.

## Rule 4
## Immediately notify the client every time something is added to the client's account balance and every time something is taken from the account balance.

## Rule 5
## Unearned fees and unexpended costs belong in the trust account until earned or spent.

Calling the fees a "retainer" or "deposit" or "advanced funds" doesn't change anything. A nonrefundable minimum retainer fee can go to your general account and be spent by you if permitted under your local rules. When the fee is earned, you must withdraw the earned fee, notifying the client of the withdrawal and the remaining balance in the account. You do not have to wait for client permission to withdraw the funds, but if the client complains about the fee taken, you must immediately return the funds to the account until the disagreement is resolved. Costs expended in accordance with your written fee agreement normally need not be returned to the account if the client complains.

## Rule 6
## Do not commingle your funds with the client funds in the trust account.

Your funds must be removed immediately upon being earned. You probably may leave a "nominal amount" of your funds in the account to cover check printing and miscellaneous charges to the account. Ask your ethics hot line how much you may keep in the account. Typically, the amount allowed, if any, is $50 to $200.

The IRS will be especially interested in whether you left earned fees in the account on December 31st to defer fees into the next taxable year.

Do not pay personal or office expenses from the trust account even if earned. Transfer the earned fees to the general account and spend from there.

## Rule 7
## Be sure you understand the exact nature of the item deposited or credited to the trust account.

Do not write checks against the deposit or make advances out of the account until you are positive the deposit is good. If the deposit bounces or is not honored, checks that clear will be cleared against the funds of other clients and you will have compounded the rules violation.

## Rule 8
## Reconcile the bank trust account monthly.

If your CPA or office manager does the reconciliation, be sure you have personally examined the reconciliation and are satisfied that your records and the bank statement reconcile to each other. Trust account responsibility cannot be delegated to anyone else. You and your license to practice are personally responsible for others' mistakes.

## Rule 9
## Reconcile and examine the individual client trust account balances monthly, and do not delay giving the clients their money.

Trust accounts should liquidate in a month or two in most cases. If the funds are in the account more than ninety days, there should be a good reason. By notifying the clients monthly of the balance in their account, the clients will normally inquire as to when they will get their money.

## Rule 10
## Be alert to third-party claims.

In some states, failure to honor a third-party lien on trust accounts is an ethics violation. In other states, only trust account disputes between the client and the lawyer are covered by ethics rules. If there is an unresolved dispute between third parties or between you and third parties over funds in the trust account, get an ethics opinion and consider interpleading the money into court.

Following these ten rules will help you avoid some of the most common trust account problems.

## TEN STEPS TO GOOD TRUST ACCOUNT RECORDS

This is a short summary of longer chapters describing mandatory trust account records and documents. Use this list for a quick review of how to maintain good trust account records.

1.  Get a copy of your current local rules and read them.

2.  Give a copy of the rules to your CPA along with a copy of this book, so the CPA can set up a "no brainer" system for your office.

3.  Be sure you reconcile everything at least monthly.

4.  It's all right to use a computer to write checks, record bank deposits, maintain balances, do reconciliations, etc., but be sure you make a hard-copy printout once a month for easy examination.

5.  Maintain a journal. The journal can be the client trust account checkbook. The starting point and main focal point in your system should be the trust account checkbook. A simple, ordinary handwritten checkbook is adequate if you record all deposits, checks, dates, and amounts and explain each item. This will be the source document for all subsequently prepared required records.

6.  Keep a client ledger. This is a trust account term, not an accounting term. It is the statutory name (in many states) for a simple running balance by client with all checks, disbursements, dates, amounts explanations, etc., on the card with a running balance calculated after each transaction.

7.  Track client balances. This is simply a list of every client trust account balance as of month's end by client name and amount. The total of this list should equal the total of all the individual ledger cards.

8.  Do regular bank reconciliations. This is nothing more than the old-fashioned bank reconciliation found on the back of most bank statements on which you reconcile cash per checkbook to cash per bank statement.

9.  Do regular triple reconciliations. To be in perfect balance, the reconciled bank balance must reconcile to the client balances total, which must reconcile to the total of all the ledger cards.

10. Your financial statements. Do not combine or include client trust account cash with other cash balances on the financial statements you give to creditors. It's not yours.

If you follow these ten steps, you should have no difficulty in producing the required documents and reports when needed.

# PART VII

---

# TRUST ACCOUNT FORMS

# TRUST ACCOUNT FORMS

The forms that follow are generic. They are intended to be examples of forms a lawyer can use to comply with local rules.

Different jurisdictions often have slightly different requirements as to form or content. A particular jurisdiction may have specific requirements as to type size or wording.

Accordingly, lawyers or firms would be wise to prepare their own set of forms based on these forms and send a set both to the local Interest On Lawyer Trust Accounts (IOLTA) authorities and to the local ethics body. It is not likely that either will "approve" or "disapprove" the forms. If a formal review and approval or disapproval were sought, it might be refused or ignored. On the other hand, a firm might get a response with suggestions. Having submitted the forms for review might help a lawyer or firm should a problem arise at a later time.

*The following forms are included in this part:*

*Notices*
1. Notice of Trust Account Disbursement
2. Notice to Client of Proposed Settlement and Disbursement of Funds
3. Notice of Trust Account Receipt-Deposit
4. Notice of Transfer of Fees and Costs from Trust Account
5. Trust Account Disbursement to Nonclient
6. Notice to Third-Party Medical Lien Claimant
7. Notice to Client Concerning Service of Process
8. Notice to Third Parties Seeking Trust Account Information

*Required Forms (typed or computer printout)*
9. Sample Client Ledger Card (also called Ledger Card Account)
10. Sample Schedule of Client Balances

*Required Forms (handwritten)*
11. Client Ledger Card
12. Schedule of Trust Account Balances (also called Summary of Client Ledgers)
13. Journal (also called Account Journal)
14. Bank Reconciliation
15. Reconciliation of Cash in Trust Accounts at 1st National Bank

**Form 1**
**NOTICE OF TRUST ACCOUNT DISBURSEMENT**
**(Trust Account Form No. 1)**

ARWEE HONEST AND HOWE
ATTORNEYS AT LAW
123 MAIN STREET
ANYTOWN, USA

Trusting Client Company
123 Lobotomy Road
Happy Valley
State of Narcosis

Re: <u>Trusting Client Realty Trust</u>

Dear Client:

Please be advised that we have this day issued our trust account check No. 27 drawn on the Left Bank of The Ohio in the amount of $97,000.19 representing your share of the proceeds of dissolution of the realty trust.

Prior to this disbursement the balance of your trust account was

|  |  |
|---|---|
|  | $ 97,000.19 |
| This disbursement | $ 97,000.19 |
|  |  |
| Balance after this disbursement | $ 00,000.00 |

cc: Client file
cc: To accompany check
cc: Trust account reconciliation

**Form 2**
**NOTICE TO CLIENT OF PROPOSED SETTLEMENT**
**AND DISBURSEMENT OF FUNDS**
**(Trust Account Form No. 2)**


ARWEE HONEST AND HOWE
ATTORNEYS AT LAW
123 MAIN STREET
ANYTOWN, USA

Ms. Hurtsobad Client
123 Compensation Syndrome Rd.
Great Settlement Township
State of Delirium

Re: <u>Hurtsobad Client vs. E. L. Diablo</u>

Dear Ms. Client:

This letter will confirm our previous telephone conversation of January 13, 19xx. We have an offer from (insurance company for Mr. Diablo) to settle your case in the gross amount of $ _____.

The gross settlement would be disbursed as follows:

Gross amount:                               $
<Less>
Property damage:                            $
Out-of-pocket costs:                        $
   Police reports
   Medical reports
   Filing and service fees
   Other
Other:                                      $
Total out-of-pocket costs:                  $_____

Our fee (as agreed):                        $
Balance:                                    $

Liens
    Dr. Patient Wait
    Huesos Quebrados Hospital
    Other
Total liens:                          $

Net to you:                       $_____

(Optional: Please understand that any other doctor bills are your responsibility and must be paid by you directly.)

**Form 3**
**NOTICE OF TRUST ACCOUNT RECEIPT-DEPOSIT**
**(Trust Account Form No. 3)**

ARWEE HONEST AND HOWE
ATTORNEYS AT LAW
123 MAIN STREET
ANYTOWN, USA

Date _____

Mr. Trusting Soul
Graybar Hotel, Suite 4376 South
Irontown

Re: <u>Soul vs. Mephistopheles</u>
    <u>Our File No. _____</u>

Dear Client:

Please be advised that we are in receipt of the following item(s) (see footnote), which will be sent to our bank for deposit or for collection and credit to our Client Trust Account in accordance with the Rules of Professional Conduct of The State Bar Act and in accordance with the Rules concerning Interest on Lawyers' Trust Accounts. (Cite the governing authority).

(Optional) We have added your endorsement under limited power of attorney in accordance with our retainer agreement.

(Optional) We have added your endorsement under the authority granted to us by you in our retainer agreement.

(Optional) We have added your endorsement under the authority granted to us by you in our billing policy memorandum.

In accordance with the rules of the Federal Reserve Bank and of the Federal Reserve District and the Interest on Lawyers' Trust Account rules and our office policies, these funds cannot be drawn upon until our account is properly credited by the drawee bank and the

Federal Reserve Clearinghouse. We will be able to write checks against these funds in 5 (five) business days.

Description of Item(s) (see footnote)

Draft No. 46238 issued by Bad Guys Auto Insurance Specialist Company in the amount of $36,994.00 as full and final settlement of claim against Mephistopheles, et al. D/A January 22, 19xx, as explained in our letter of January 2, 19xx.

| | |
|---|---|
| Balance of your account prior to deposit | $ 12,946.38 |
| This deposit-collection | $ 36,994.00 |
| | |
| Balance of your account after credit by bank | $ 49,940.38 |

Note: I recommend a separate notice for each receipt to be able to reconstruct the account at a later time if needed. You may combine multiple items if you wish.

cc: Client file
cc: Trust account reconciliation file
cc: Duplicate deposit ticket

**Form 4**
**NOTICE OF TRANSFER OF FEES AND COSTS**
**FROM TRUST ACCOUNT**
**(Trust Account Form No. 4)**

ARWEE HONEST AND HOWE
ATTORNEYS AT LAW
123 MAIN STREET
ANYTOWN, USA

Mr. Arthur Goodpay
Seventh Happiness Inn
99 No Sweat Road
Good Hands

Dear Mr. Goodpay:

In accordance with our agreement, we have this day transferred the sum of $3,123.46 from our client trust account to our office account by our client trust account check No. 329. This transfer represents earned fees of $2900.00 and cost reimbursement of $223.46 as set forth on the accompanying monthly statement for services rendered during the month of March 19xx.

| | |
|---|---|
| Balance of your account before transfer | $7,500.00 |
| This transfer | $3,123.46 |
| Balance of your account after transfer | $4,376.54 |

cc: Client file
cc: Trust account reconciliation file

## Form 5
## TRUST ACCOUNT DISBURSEMENT TO NONCLIENT
### (Trust Account Form No. 5)

ARWEE HONEST AND HOWE
ATTORNEYS AT LAW
123 MAIN STREET
ANYTOWN, USA

Ms. Mary M. Contrary
123 Quite Contrary Garden Road
Cockleshell Town

Re: <u>Payment for claim against Mr. Goodguy</u>

Dear Ms. Contrary:

Enclosed herewith is our client trust account check No. 77 drawn on the Sunset Strip Bank in the amount of $11,000.00 representing payment to you in full for a release of your claims against our client Mr. Goodguy as set forth in the Settlement Agreement of July 27, 19xx, previously executed by you.

We wish to repeat that we are not your attorneys and have not given you any legal advice and you have not relied on legal advice from us in arriving at your settlement agreement.

This check can immediately be deposited or negotiated by you.

Very truly yours,

cc: Client
cc: Client file
cc: Trust account reconciliation file

Note: Be careful that unsophisticated unrepresented clients do not rely on you, erroneously believing that you are protecting "everybody" and their money.

## Form 6
## NOTICE TO THIRD-PARTY MEDICAL LIEN CLAIMANT
### (Trust Account Form No. 6)

ARWEE HONEST AND HOWE
ATTORNEYS AT LAW
123 MAIN STREET
ANYTOWN, USA

Will Waitfor Yew, M.D.
456 Pill Hill Medical Center
Palindrome Syndrome Village,
State of Remission

Re: <u>Jones v. Smith Date/Accident January 13, 19xx</u>

Dear Dr. Yew:

We are about to settle (We have settled) the case of our mutual client/patient Arthur Jones for injuries arising out of his accident of January 13, 19xx.

According to the last information received by us from your offices the sum of $xxxx.xx is due to your offices and will be paid to you at the time of disbursal of funds.

(Optional) We are appreciative of the fact that you have reduced your lien to $xxxx.xx to make it possible for us to settle the case.

(Optional) According to our client you have reduced your bill to $xxxx.xx in order to make it possible for us to settle the case.

(Optional) According to our client/patient you and he have agreed that we should send you $xxx.xx of the settlement funds and you and he have made your own arrangements for payment of the balance.

After disbursement of the settlement you will have to look directly to Mr. Jones for future amounts.

We would appreciate your signing or marking the enclosed copy of this letter and mailing or faxing it back to our offices indicating that it is correct so that we may pay you the sum of $xxx.xx from the settlement.

If we do not hear from you in ten days, we shall assume the balance is correct. (Optional if permitted under the terms of the lien.)

Arwee Honest and Howe


By Ima Straightarrow

To Arwee Honest and Howe:

You may send us the sum of $xxx.xx as set forth in the above letter in discharge of our lien.

_____          _____

Will Waitfor Yew, M.D.                            Date

cc: Happy client
cc: Trust account records

## Form 7
## NOTICE TO CLIENT CONCERNING SERVICE OF PROCESS
### (Trust Account Form No. 7)

ARWEE HONEST AND HOWE
ATTORNEYS AT LAW
123 MAIN STREET
ANYTOWN, USA

R. Good Client
Graybar Hotel Suite 4372
P.O. Box 1040
Clubfed Farms & Tennis Resort
Redemption

Re: <u>Service of process</u>

Dear Ms. Client:

We have been served with a subpoena duces tecum/summons to produce information from our trust account as to financial transactions concerning your affairs. A copy of that process in enclosed. We are also enclosing a copy of our response.

You have a right, if you wish, to assert various privileges including the attorney-client privilege, the privilege against self-incrimination, and the privilege against unreasonable search and seizure as well as certain rights under the state and federal consumer privacy acts.

Unless you waive these rights we will assert them for you.

(Optional if permitted.) Should we proceed to further resist providing information we will have to charge you for services to be rendered.

(Optional if permitted.) Under the terms of our employment agreement of January 13, 19xx, you will be billed for our services in resisting the voluntary providing of information. We estimate our fees will run between $xxxx and $zzzz for resisting at this first level. We have based our estimate on information known to us at this time.

(Optional if applicable.) We have asked our State Bar Ethics Counsel the extent, if at all, we must resist process.

We are not aware of any particular reason you would not wish us to voluntarily provide this information without delay or cost, but we need to know your wishes.

Please communicate with us immediately.

Very truly yours,

Arwee Honest and Howe
By: I.M. Ethical

Enclosures:
1. Copy of subpoena
2. Copy of our response

**Form 8**
**NOTICE TO THIRD PARTIES SEEKING**
**TRUST ACCOUNT INFORMATION**
**(Trust Account Form No. 8)**

ARWEE HONEST AND HOWE
ATTORNEYS AT LAW
123 MAIN STREET
ANYTOWN, USA

Ketchum, Holdem and Skinnum
Attorneys for I.M. Cheap, Defendant

U.R. Nosey, Special Investigator
Big Brother Section
We're Here To Help You Bureau
Friendly Government Agency

Re: Request for trust account information as
contained in your summons or subpoena

You have requested trust account information concerning R. Good Client.

Please be advised that we are ethically prohibited from supplying the information requested and we are obligated to protect the confidences of all of our clients whether or not you claim to be interested in their legal and financial affairs.

Accordingly we must respectfully decline to provide you with the information demanded unless the client is willing to voluntarily and knowingly waive any rights they may have to maintain confidences and attorney-client privilege. We are in the process of communicating with our client (former client) and we will promptly notify you if the affected client(s) authorize release of information.

Under local procedure we must respectfully [move to quash your Subpoena] [Resist enforcement of Summons] (describe the appropriate process).

You indicated that you feel that you ultimately might be successful in a judicial proceeding and for that reason we should voluntarily provide you with what you believe you could get by court order.

We would remind you that your situation and our situation are similar. You are in possession of information which you cannot voluntarily provide us under appropriate state and federal privacy and consumer laws, even though this information could be obtained pursuant to applicable state and federal Freedom of Information Acts and consumer laws. We are in a comparable situation. We cannot give you confidential information voluntarily that you might or might not get on court application.

We respectfully must inform you that if you wish to proceed further, we will respectfully assert attorney-client privileges and confidences not only as to the person(s) for whom you seek information, but for all clients whose names or legal matters might become known to you during any investigation.

We will notify the court we are asserting attorney-client privileges and all other privileges which might be applicable as to all clients and ask the court to do an in camera inspection of all trust account data to frame an order to appropriately redact information as to other clients and information as to the subject which would be confidential and privileged to the clients or persons concerning whom you wish information.

Please let us know whether you wish to continue to seek judicial or administrative process to obtain trust account information.

As previously indicated, should the client voluntarily waive privilege we will promptly notify you.

Very truly yours,


Arwee Honest and Howe
By: I.M. Ethical

## Form 9
## SAMPLE CLIENT LEDGER CARD
### (Also Called Ledger Card Account)

ARWEE HONEST AND HOWE
ATTORNEYS AT LAW
CLIENT TRUST ACCOUNT—MISSISSIPPI WEST BANK
CLIENT LEDGER CARD

CLIENT                       S. Simon
MATTER                 Sale of pie and bakery facility
RESPONSIBLE ATTORNEY    Dudley Doright

| Date | Check# | Payee/Source/Memo | Check | Deposits | Balance |
|------|--------|-------------------|-------|----------|---------|
| 01/13/9x | | From S. Simon | | | |
| | | Deposit for fees/costs | | 5000. | 5000. |
| 01/13/9x | | From R. Hero | | | |
| | | Deposit for lien payoff | | 20,000. | 25,000. |
| 02/28/9x | 1436 | January fees and costs | 3300. | | 21,700. |
| 03/10/9x | | Additional deposit | | | |
| | | fees and costs | | 3300. | 25,000. |
| 03/26/9x | | From M. Pieman | | | |
| | | Purchase price | | 100,000. | 125,000. |
| 03/07/9x | 1496 | February fees and costs | 5000. | | 120,000. |
| 03/07/9x | 1497 | S. Simon | 120,000. | | 0 |
| 03/07/9x | | Balance of account | | | —0— |

## Form 10
## SAMPLE SCHEDULE OF CLIENT BALANCES

ARWEE HONEST AND HOWE
ATTORNEYS AT LAW
CLIENT TRUST ACCOUNT—MISSISSIPPI WEST BANK
SCHEDULE OF CLIENT BALANCES

AS OF JANUARY 31, 19XX

NOTE: In some jurisdictions this is called a "journal" for the bank account

In accountants' terminology, this list of the balances belonging to each client in the particular client trust account would be called the subsidiary ledger or the detail and would reconcile to the adjusted bank balance in the bank account.

In some jurisdictions this would be equivalent to a listing of all the client individual ledgers where the money was in this particular bank account.

There should be a separate list for each bank account maintained as a client's trust account if the law firm has more than one client trust account.

| Client Name and Matter | Balance as of January 31,19xx |
|---|---|
| B. Able—Sale of business | $25,000.00 |
| Sa Boy—Adoption | $1,000.00 |
| Grate Collectors—Jones | $550.00 |
| Grate Collectors—Squeezed | $1,975.00 |
| Grate Collectors—Multiple matters | $9,476.22 |
| Sheeza Dear adv. A Schnook—Auto accident | $38,000.00 |
| Unhappy Client—Disputed fees | $2,500.00 |
| Firm Funds—For administrative bank charges and checks | $200.00 |
| Good Guy v. Bad Guy—Advanced fees deposit | $5,000.00 |

Good Guy v. Bad Guy—Advanced costs deposit     $1,000.00
Departed Client—Probate house sale     $235,000.00 *

Total in accounts as reconciled to bank account     $319,701.22 **

* One should immediately raise the question of whether there is adequate insurance and additionally whether the funds are likely to be held for a substantial period of time so that they should be placed in a non-IOLTA account to get the interest to the client.

** Even after removing the $235,000 to get the interest to the client, the lawyer should inquire of the bank in writing whether the entire account is insured for $100,000 or whether each client's portion is insured for $100,000.

# FORM 11
## CLIENT LEDGER CARD
## CLIENT VS. DEFENDANT

| ACCOUNT NO. | 98-467 | | NAME | | | Arthur P. Client | | | | |
|---|---|---|---|---|---|---|---|---|---|---|
| SHEET NO. | 1 | | ADDRESS | | | | | | | |

| DATE | | ITEMS | FOLIO | √ | DEBITS | √ | CREDITS | DR. OR CR. | BALANCE |
|---|---|---|---|---|---|---|---|---|---|
| Jan. 14 | 9x | Settlement check from ABC insurance | | | | | | | |
| | | company for Defendant | | | | | 2 2 5 0 0 — | | 2 2 5 0 0 — |
| Jan. 8 | 9x | Settlement check from XYZ insurance | | | | | | | |
| | | company for Defendant's employer | | | | | 2 2 5 0 0 — | | 4 5 0 0 0 — |
| | | | | | | | | | |
| Feb 2 | 9x | Dr. Smith—Medical lien ck #908 | | | 8 5 0 — | | | | |
| | | LST Hospital—Medical lien ck #909 | | | 3 0 0 0 | | | | |
| | | Arwee Honest & Howe—Cost | | | | | | | |
| | | Remb #910 | | | 1 5 0 | | | | |
| | | Arwee Honest & Howe—Fees | | | | | | | |
| | | (25%) #911 | | | 1 1 2 5 0 | | | | |
| | | R. Good Client—Net    #912 | | | 2 9 7 5 0 | | | | — 0 — |
| | | | | | | | | | |
| | | | | | | | | | |
| | | | | | | | | | |
| | | | | | | | | | |
| | | | | | | | | | |
| | | | | | | | | | |
| | | | | | | | | | |

# FORM 12
## SCHEDULE OF TRUST ACCOUNT BALANCES
## (ALSO CALLED SUMMARY OF CLIENT LEDGERS)
## FOR PERIOD ENDING 6-30-XX

| ACCOUNT NO. | | | | NAME | | | | | | |
|---|---|---|---|---|---|---|---|---|---|---|
| SHEET NO. | | | | ADDRESS | | | | | | |

| DATE | ITEMS | FOLIO | √ | DEBITS | √ | CREDITS | DR. OR CR. | BALANCE |
|---|---|---|---|---|---|---|---|---|
| | Jones adv Smith Balance | | | | | 3 0 0 0 | | |
| | Smith vs. Buick (costs advanced by client) | | | | | 2 0 0 0 | | |
| | Jones adv Smith –New– D/A 1/10/xx | | | | | 1 0 0 0 | | |
| | Hackoff vs. Insurance | | | | | 7 0 0 0 | | |
| | | | | | | | | |
| | Balance of Client Ledger | | | | | 1 3 0 0 0 — | | |
| | | | | | | | | |

# FORM 13
# JOURNAL
# (ALSO CALLED ACCOUNT JOURNAL)
# JUNE 1 TO JUNE 30

| NAME Client Trust Account | | ACCOUNT NO. | | | | | | | |
|---|---|---|---|---|---|---|---|---|---|
| ADDRESS 1st Natl. Bank | | Checks | SHEET NO. Deposits | | | | Running | | |
| DATE | CLIENT | DESCRIPTION | FOLIO | √ | DEBITS | √ | CREDITS | DR. OR CR. | BALANCE |
| 6-1 | | Balance Forward | | | | | | | 27000 |
| 6-3 | Jones adv Smith | Medical liens | | | 3000 | | | | 24000 |
| | check #108 √ | Cost reimbursement | | | 1000 | | | | 23000 |
| | check #109 √ | Fee reimbursement | | | 9000 | | | | 14000 |
| | check #110 √ | To Jones | | | 12000 | | | | 2000 |
| 6-14 | Spencer Probate | Sale of House | | | | | 100000 | 1 | 102000 |
| | check #111 | To Broker Smith | | | 3000 | | | | 99000 |
| | Filing fees & costs | Filing fees reimbursement | | | 375 | | | | 98625 |
| | Fees | | | | 1000 | | | | 97625 |
| | To Seller | | | | 90000 | | | | 7625 |
| | | | | | 94375 | | | | |

# FORM 14
# BANK RECONCILIATION
# JUNE 30 19XX

| ACCOUNT NO. | 143816 | NAME | Client Trust Account |
| SHEET NO. | | ADDRESS | 1st National Bank, Anytown, U.S.A. |

| DATE | ITEMS | FOLIO | √ | DEBITS | √ | CREDITS | DR. OR CR. | BALANCE |
|---|---|---|---|---|---|---|---|---|
| | Balance Per Bank Statement 6-30-19xx | | | | | | | 1 1 5 0 3 — |
| | | | | | | | | |
| | Add: Deposit of 6-25 in transit | | | | | 4 5 0 0 — | | |
| | 6-29 in transit | | | | | 6 5 0 0 — | | |
| | Total deposits in transit 6-30-19xx | | | | 1 1 0 0 0 | | | 1 1 0 0 0 |
| | Less: Outstanding checks not cleared | | | | | | | 2 2 5 0 3 |
| | #476 6-20-xx | | | | | 7 5 0 0 | | |
| | #495 6-29-xx | | | | | 3 0 0 0 | | |
| | #301 5-20-xx | | | | | 2 0 0 0 | | |
| | Total outstanding checks 6-30-xx | | | | 1 2 5 0 0 | | < | 1 2 5 0 0 > |
| | Adjusted Bank Balance | | | | | | 8 | 1 0 0 0 3 |
| | | | | | | | | |
| | Balance per check stubs 6-30-xx | | | | | | | 1 0 0 0 3 |
| | | | | | | | | |
| | Difference = | | | | | | | — 0 — |
| | | | | | | | | |
| | | | | | | | | |
| | | | | | | | | |

# FORM 15
## RECONCILIATION OF CASH IN TRUST ACCOUNTS
## AT 1ST NATIONAL BANK
## JAN. 31, 19XX

| ACCOUNT NO. | | | NAME | | | | | | | |
|---|---|---|---|---|---|---|---|---|---|---|
| SHEET NO. | | | ADDRESS | | | | | | | |

| DATE | TRUST ACCOUNT BALANCES | FOLIO | √ | DEBITS | √ | CREDITS | DR. OR CR. | BALANCE |
|---|---|---|---|---|---|---|---|---|
| A. | Balance per bank at January 31, 19xx | | | | | | $ | 3 0 0 0 0 |
| | add: Deposit in transit Jan. 31, 19xx | | | | | | | |
| | not on statement | | | | | | | 1 5 0 0 0 |
| | Balance per bank as adjusted Jan 31, 19xx | | | | | | $ | 4 5 0 0 0 |
| | | | | | | | | |
| B. | Trust Account Balances | | | | | | | |
| | Balance: Client vs. Defendant | | | | | | | |
| | Jan. 31, 19xx | | | | | | $ | 3 0 0 0 0 |
| | Smith fee deposit | | | | | | | 1 5 0 0 0 |
| | | | | | | | | |
| | Balance per client schedule of balances | | | | | | $ | 4 5 0 0 0 |
| | | | | | | | | |
| | Difference | | | | | | | 0 |

# ENDNOTES

## PART I
## UNDERSTANDING TRUST ACCOUNT PRINCIPLES

### The Importance of Trust Account Management

1. *See, e.g.,* ABA Model Standards for Imposing Lawyer Sanctions, Standard 4.11, which provides for disbarment for knowing conversion of client property with injury or potential injury to client; Chefsky v. State Bar, 36 Cal. 3d 116, 123, 680 P.2d 82 (1984), which held disbarment appropriate for lawyer's gross negligence in dealing with client property.

2. State *ex rel.* Oklahoma Bar Ass'n v. Dunlap, 880 P.2d 364, 368 (Okla. 1994), held that the mere act of allowing the level of a client's trust account to fall below the amount held on behalf of clients, without more, constitutes mishandling of client funds.

3. Discipline: *In re* Konopka, 596 A.2d 733, 739–40 (N.J. 1991). Civil liability: Eatinger v. Johnson, 887 P.2d 231, 235 (Mont. 1994), *reh'g denied*; Lurz v. Panek, 123 Ill. Dec. 200, 527 N.E.2d 663, 667–68, 172 Ill. App. 3d 915 (Ill. App. 2 Dist. 1988).

4. Disbarment: *In re* Godfrey, 583 A.2d 692, 693 (D.C. App. 1990). Civil liability: Avianca, Inc. v. Corriea, 705 F. Supp. 666, 682 (D.D.C. 1989). Criminal liability: *In re* Wright, 10 Cal. 3d 374, 110 Cal. Rptr. 340, 515 P.2d 292 (Cal. 1973).

### Common Transactions Requiring Trust Accounts

1. State Bar *ex rel.* Oklahoma Bar Ass'n v. Miskovsky, 824 P.2d 1090, 1097–98 (Okla. 1991).

2. Galardi v. State Bar, 43 Cal. 3d 383, 288 Cal. Rptr. 774 (1987).

3. Reeck v. Polk, 257 N.W.2d 698, 699, 269 Mich. 262 (Mich. 1934); *In re* Tidball, 503 N.W.2d 850 (S.D. 1993).

4. State *ex rel.* Nebraska State Bar Ass'n v. Hendrickson, 295 N.W. 148, 139 Neb. 522 (Neb. 1941).

5. *In re* Broderick, 3 Cal. State Bar Ct. Rptr. 138, 153–54 (Cal. Review Dept. 1994).

6. MODEL RULES Rule 1.15(a) does not expressly state that advances for costs should be placed in a client trust account. However, the ABA MODEL RULES, at page 258, states that the rule was intended to cover advanced costs. In many states, the requirement of placing advanced costs into a client trust account is mandated by specific rule or case law. *See, e.g.,* Aronin v. State Bar, 52 Cal. 3d 276, 284, 276 Cal. Rptr. 153 (Cal. 1990). *Contra* MODEL CODE DR 9-102(A) expressly exempts advances for costs and expenses from deposit into the client trust account. Also note that client's reimbursement of costs already advanced by the lawyer need not go into the client trust account. Louisiana v. Williams, 512 So. 2d 404 (La. 1987) *reh'g denied.*

7. MODEL RULES Rule 1.15(a) does not expressly state that advances for fees should be placed in a client trust account. In many states, the requirement to place advanced fees in the trust account is established by specific rule or case law. *See, e.g., In re* Biggs, 864 P.2d 1310, 1316, 318 Or. 281 (Or. 1994); *In re* Gustafson, 493 N.W.2d 551, 553–54 (Minn. 1992). Note exception: Nonrefundable or true retainers are earned when received and need not be placed in a client trust account. *In re* Gustafson, 493 N.W.2d 551, 553–54 (Minn. 1992).

8. *See, e.g., In re* Biggs, 864 P.2d 1310, 1316, 318 Or. 281 (Or. 1994); *In re* Gustafson, 493 N.W.2d 551, 553–54 (Minn. 1992). *Contra* re minimum fee in a criminal case: *In re* Jackson, 867 P.2d 278, 280, 254 Kan. 406 (Kan. 1994).

9. MODEL RULES Rule 1.15(a). *Contra* re deposits for costs and expenses: MODEL CODE DR 9-102(A).

10. MODEL RULES Rule 1.15(c); MODEL CODE DR 9-102(A).

11. *In re* Ortega, 688 P.2d 329, 330 (N.M. 1984); Rhode Island State Bar Formal Ethics Op. No. 93-16.

12. Galardi v. State Bar, 43 Cal. 3d 383, 288 Cal. Rptr. 774 (1987).

13. Sternlieb v. State Bar, 52 Cal. 3d 317 (Cal. 1992).

14. State *ex rel.* Oklahoma Bar Ass'n v. Johnston, 863 P.2d 1136, 1144 (Okla. 1993) (payments withheld for client's medical bills converted); *In re* Respondent P, 2 Cal. State Bar Ct. Rptr. 622, 627, 630 (1993 Cal. State Bar Ct. Rev. Dep't) (settlement funds to pay statutory lien).

15. *In re* Pollack, 536 N.Y.S.2d 437, 438–39 (N.Y. Sup. Ct. App. Div. 1st Dep't 1989) (estate funds).

16. State Bar *ex rel.* Oklahoma Bar Ass'n v. Miskovsky, 824 P.2d 1090, 1095, 1096–97 (Okla. 1991), involved client funds for a criminal defendant's fine, victim compensation assessment, and assessed court costs.

17. MODEL RULES Rule 1.15 (a) & (c); MODEL CODE DR 9-102(A).

### Differing ABA and State Rules

1. Washington, D.C., Rules of Professional Conduct, Rule 1.15(d).
2. Title 22, New York Codes, Rules & Regulations (NYCRR), § 1200.46 [DR 9-102].

## A Summary of Common-Law Background and Origins of Trust Account Rules

1. Financial General Bankshares, Inc. v. Metzger, 680 F.2d 768, 772–73, 777–78 (D.C. Cir. 1982).
2. Bonanza Motors, Inc. v. Webb, 657 P.2d 1102, 1104, 104 Idaho 234 (Id. App. 1983).
3. HENRY S. DRINKER, LEGAL ETHICS 89–96 (Columbia University Press 1953).
4. *See, e.g.,* CAL. PROBATE CODE §§ 16002–16004 (incorporating former CAL. CIVIL CODE §§ 1118, 2229, 2231, and 2235 regarding the duty of loyalty, highest good faith of a trustee, and dealings between a trustee and beneficiary).
5. *In re* Respondent P, 2 Cal. State Bar Ct. Rptr. 622, 630 (1993 Cal. State Bar Ct. Rev. Dep't).
6. Bonanza Motors, Inc. v. Webb, 657 P.2d 1102, 1104, 104 Idaho 234 (Id. App. 1983); ABA/BNA LAWYER'S MANUAL ON PROFESSIONAL CONDUCT at 45:1104–05, 45:1106 [hereinafter ABA/BNA MANUAL].
7. 7 AM. JUR. 2D, *Attys at Law* § 53, at 112–13; 1993 Supp. at 66–68.
8. MALLEN & SMITH, LEGAL MALPRACTICE (3rd ed. 1989) at 630–33.
9. MALLEN & SMITH, LEGAL MALPRACTICE at 1993 Supp., 281.
10. Padco, Inc. v. Kinney & Lange, 444 N.W.2d 889, 891 (Minn. App. 1989).
11. Condren v. Grace, 783 F. Supp. 178, 179–80, (S.D.N.Y. 1992).

### Interest on Lawyers' Trust Accounts (IOLTA)

1. ABA/BNA MANUAL at 45:201–05 (1991); MODEL RULES at 254.
2. ABA/BNA MANUAL at 45:201 (1991).
3. MODEL RULES at 254; Kansas State Bar Ass'n Op. No. 94-12 (Nov. 29, 1994) opines that an attorney may maintain client funds in a non-interest-bearing client trust account with the client's consent.
4. Some states require that all client funds go into some form of an interest-bearing client trust account. Committee on Professional Ethics and Conduct of the Iowa State Bar Ass'n v. Clauss, 445 N.W.2d 758, 760 (Iowa 1989).
5. *Matter of Interest on Trust Accounts: Petition to Amend Rules Regulating the Florida Bar,* 538 So. 2d 448, 453 (Fla. 1989); Carroll v. State Bar of California, 166 Cal. App. 3d 1193, 213 Cal. Rptr. 305 (1985), *cert. denied,* 106 S. Ct. 142 (U.S. S. Ct. 1983).

6. MODEL RULES at 254.

7. *See, e.g.,* Rule 4-100(A), Rules of Professional Conduct of the State Bar of California; CAL. BUS. & PROF. CODE § 6212(a).

8. California Supreme Court Order filed December 31, 1982, regarding CAL. BUS. & PROF. CODE § 6212.

9. At least fourteen jurisdictions require bank notification of overdrafts in client trust accounts (including California, Connecticut, Florida, Idaho, Maryland, Minnesota, Montana, New Jersey, New York, North Carolina, Rhode Island, Vermont, Virginia, and Washington, D.C.). ABA/BNA MANUAL at 45:1003–04.

10. *See, e.g.,* CAL. BUS. & PROF. CODE § 6091.1 subd. (a).

## No Delegation of Trust Account Responsibility

1. Illustrative cases include the following: In Louisiana State Bar Ass'n v. Keys, 567 So. 2d 588, 589–90, 593 (La. 1009), a secretary/office manager of fifteen years made unauthorized transfers of funds from the client trust account to the lawyer's operating account whenever the operating account fell below a certain amount. The court found that the lawyer failed to supervise the secretary properly and imposed thirty days actual suspension. In *In re* Barker, 556 A.2d 1190, 1191–92, 1194, 115 N.J. 30 (N.J. 1989), a bookkeeper's error in reporting amount in a client trust account resulted in a $1,934.44 shortfall. The court found failure to supervise the bookkeeper properly and gave a public reprimand. Louisiana Bar Ass'n v. Lindsay, 553 So. 2d 807 (La. 1989), found that the attorney must oversee an accountant's work and bear ultimate responsibility for conversion of client's money. In *In re* Galbasini, 163 Ariz. 120, 124, 786 P.2d 971, 975 (Ariz. 1990), a management firm hired by a lawyer to supervise non-lawyer employees failed to supervise the employees handling of settlement funds properly. The court held that the lawyer had a duty to supervise the management firm's failure of supervision and imposed discipline. Bohna v. Hughe, 828 P.2d 745 (Al. 1992); Meyers v. Aragona, 318 A.2d 263 (Md. Ct. App. 1974); Rubin Quinn Moss Heaney & Patterson v. Kennel, 832 F. Supp. 922, 932–33 (E.D. Pa. 1993); Blackmon v. Hale, 1 Cal. 3d 548, 83 Cal. Rptr. 194, 463 P.2d 418 (1970), address a partner's vicarious liability for the misappropriation of client funds by a fellow partner or associate.

2. In New York, no lay-employee or other layperson can be a signatory to a client trust account. N.Y. Ct. Rules § 1200.46(e), DR 9-102, subd. E.

3. *In re* Struthers, 877 P.2d 789, 793 (Ariz. 1994), an attorney routinely signed blank checks, leaving to lay-employees the decision of how much to pay clients for their portions of settlements.

## A Lawyer Can Be Disciplined Even If No One Is "Hurt"

1. ABA ANNOTATED MODEL RULES OF PROFESSIONAL CONDUCT (1992) at 257–58 [hereinafter MODEL RULES].

2. *In re* Brown, 427 S.E.2d 645, 646, 310 S.C. 463 (1993).

3. *In re* Draper, 317 A.2d 106, 107–09 (Del. 1974) (real estate proceeds paid back with interest).

4. *In re* Barlow, 657 A.2d 1197, 1199–2000, 1201, 140 N.J. 191 (N.J. 1995).

5. *In re* Peek, 359 S.E.2d 677, 257 Ga. 349 (Ga. 1987).

6. *In re* Moras, 619 A.2d 1007, 1010–11, 131 N.J. 164 (N.J. 1993) (advancing funds from clients' trust account to accommodate clients where the draft or check has not yet cleared; exception: real estate or commercial closings).

7. MODEL RULES Rule 1.15(A); ABA MODEL CODE OF PROFESSIONAL RESPONSIBILITY DR 9-102(A) [hereinafter MODEL CODE]; Attorney Grievance Comm'n v. Kemp, 496 A.2d 672, 303 Md. 664 (Md. 1985) (attorney deposited client funds into personal account because he had not yet received clients' trust account checks on newly opened clients' trust account).

8. *In re* Lamb, 585 A.2d 326, 327 (N.J. 1991) (failure to maintain client ledger cards); MODEL RULES Rule 1.15 (b); MODEL CODE DR 9-102(B)(3); Attorney Grievance Comm'n of Maryland v. Sliffman, 625 A.2d 314, 319, 330 Md. 515 (Md. 1993) (failure to maintain journal or ledger cards).

9. *In re* Sawyer, 98 Wash. 2d 584, 656 P.2d 503 (1983).

10. Louisiana State Bar Ass'n v. Keys, 567 So. 2d 588, 589–90, 593 (La. 1009); *In re* Barker, 556 A.2d 1190, 1191–92, 1194, 115 N.J. 30 (N.J. 1989).

11. *In re* Pollack, 536 N.Y.S.2d 437, 438–39 (N.Y. Sup. Ct. App. Div. 1st Dep't 1989) (partner liable for the associate's placement of assets of estate into non-escrow passbook savings account that contained personal funds and office operating expenses).

12. *In re* Fleischer, 508 A.2d 1115, 102 N.J. 440 (N.J. 1986).

13. *In re* Lamb, 585 A.2d 326, 327 (N.J. 1991) (failure to produce records after audit request).

14. *In re* Respondent P, 2 Cal. State Bar Ct. Rptr. 622, 627, 630 (1993 Cal. State Bar Ct. Rev. Dep't).

## The Mechanics of a Trust Account Investigation

1. At least eight jurisdictions (including Delaware, Iowa, Nebraska, New Hampshire, New Jersey, New York [First and Second Departments] North Carolina, and Washington) have random client trust account audit programs. ABA/BNA MANUAL at 45:1003. Note: Many states have adopted a probable cause audit procedure. *See, e.g.,* CAL. BUS. & PROF. CODE § 6091.

2. At least fourteen jurisdictions require bank notification of overdrafts in client trust accounts (including California, Connecticut, Florida, Idaho, Maryland, Minnesota, Montana, New Jersey, New York, North Carolina, Rhode Island, Vermont, Virginia, and Washington, D.C.). ABA/BNA MANUAL at 45:1003–04. Most states have adopted a probable cause audit procedure.

3. MODEL RULES Rule 8.3; MODEL CODE DR 1-103(A).

4. ABA MODEL CODE OF JUDICIAL CONDUCT Canon 3(D)(2) (1990); Former ABA MODEL CODE OF JUDICIAL CONDUCT Canon 3(B)(3).

5. ABA/BNA MANUAL at 45:1003–04.

## Typical State Rules Concerning Records

1. At least seventeen jurisdictions (including Arizona, California, Delaware, Florida, Idaho, Iowa, Maine, Maryland, Minnesota, Nebraska, New Jersey, North Carolina, Virginia, Washington, and Wisconsin) have adopted some type of mandatory record-keeping rule. *See also* ABA MODEL RECORD KEEPING RULE adopted February 1993. Some states also require that lawyers submit an annual verification or certification of compliance with the record-keeping requirement.

2. ABA/BNA MANUAL at 45:1005.

## PART II
## THE BASICS OF TRUST ACCOUNT MANAGEMENT

### Have a Trust Account

1. Attorney Grievance Comm'n v. Kemp, 496 A.2d 672, 303 Md. 664 (Md. 1985) (attorney deposited client funds into personal account because he had not yet received clients' trust account checks on newly opened clients' trust account.) In State *ex rel.* Oklahoma Bar Ass'n v. Dunlap, 880 P.2d 364, 368 (Okla. 1994), the attorney did not have a trust account when he received funds on behalf of the client, so he deposited the funds in his operating account and was thereafter disciplined.

### Where to Open and Keep the Trust Account

1. *See, e.g.,* Rule 4-100(A), Rules of Professional Conduct of the State Bar of California; CAL. BUS. & PROF. CODE § 6212(a).

2. California Supreme Court Order filed December 31, 1982, regarding CAL. BUS. & PROF. CODE § 6212.

3. *See, e.g., In re* Weisman, 531 N.Y.S.2d 255, 139 A.D.2d 249 (N.Y.A.D. 1 Dep't 1988); MODEL RULES Rule 1.15(a); MODEL CODE DR 9-102(A).

4. MODEL RULES Rule 1.15(a) permits a client to direct a lawyer to place the funds elsewhere. Rule 4-100(A), Rules of Professional Conduct of the State Bar of California, requires funds to be deposited in another designated client trust account in a jurisdiction wherein the client or the client's business has a substantial relationship. MODEL CODE DR 9-102(A) does not expressly permit the client to direct an alternative depository for funds belonging to that client.

5. *See, e.g.,* CAL. BUS. & PROF. CODE § 6211 suggests that the California Supreme Court could designate other financial institutions in which both IOLTA and non-IOLTA trust funds could be deposited. The California Supreme Court Order filed December 31, 1982, permits only IOLTA funds to be placed in other types of financial institutions besides banks. Rule 4-100(A), Rules of Professional Conduct of the State Bar of California, thus requires non-IOLTA accounts to be placed in banks.

## Have a Clients Safe Deposit Box or a Fireproof Safe

1. MODEL RULES Rule 1.15(b); MODEL CODE DR 9-102(B)(2).

2. For example, bonds must be maintained in a safe deposit box. (South Dakota State Bar Ethics Op. No. 91-20.) An attorney who loses a check or draft that contains client funds is culpable of violating this rule. *In re* Broderick, 3 Cal. State Bar Ct. Rptr. 138, 154–55 (Cal. St. Bar Ct. Rev. Dep't 1994). *But see* Lister v. State Bar, 51 Cal. 3d 1121, 275 Cal. Rptr. 802, 807–08 (Cal. 1990), wherein the California Supreme Court refused to find an attorney culpable for leaving a negotiable IRS check payable to an estate in his file for over one and one-half years.

## The General Rules of Fees and Trust Accounts

1. MODEL RULES Rule 1.15(a); MODEL CODE DR 9-102(A); New Hampshire State Bar Ethics Op. No. 1990-91.

2. *In re* Gambino, 619 N.Y.S.2d 305, 205 A.D.2d 212 (N.Y.A.D. 2d Dep't 1994) (attorney disciplined for retaining attorney's fees in clients' trust account).

3. Archer v. State, 548 S.W.2d 71, 73–74, 94 A.L.R. 837 (Tex. Civ. App. 1977) (client consent does not permit attorney to commingle client funds with personal funds).

4. In New York, nonrefundable retainers are prohibited. *In re* Cooperman, 611 N.Y.S.2d 465, 83 N.Y.2d 465, 633 N.E.2d 1069 (N.Y. 1994).

5. New Hampshire State Bar Ethics Op. No. 1990-91 opines that nonrefundable retainers are earned when paid and received and therefore should be placed in the lawyer's operating account, provided they are supported by a written retainer agreement. *See also In re* Biggs, 864 P.2d 1310, 1316, 318 Or. 281 (Or. 1994); *In re* Gustafson, 493 N.W.2d 551, 553–54 (Minn. 1992).

6. *But see In re* Cacioppo, 2 Cal. State Bar Ct. Rptr. 128, 146 (Cal. State Bar Ct. Review Dep't 1992), which held that a lawyer must present a bill for legal services to the client before the lawyer withdraws the fees from client's trust account funds.

7. Some states hold that a lawyer must give a client an accounting for charges against advanced fees. *In re* Fonte, 2 Cal. State Bar Ct. Rptr. 752, 758 (Cal. State Bar Ct. Review Dep't 1994), held that there is a duty to account for expenditure of advances for fees.

8. MODEL CODE DR 9-102(A); Rhode Island State Bar Formal Op. 92-12; *In re* Fonte, 2 Cal. State Bar Ct. Rptr. 752, 758 (Cal. State Bar Ct. Review Dep't 1994), held that if fees taken from advanced fees are disputed, they must be replaced into the client trust account until the dispute is resolved.

## Retainer Fees and Trust Accounts

1. *See, e.g.,* Rule 3-700(D)(2), Rules of Professional Conduct of the State Bar of California; Louisiana Bar Ass'n v. Fish, 562 So. 2d 892 (La. 1990).

2. *In re* Gustafson, 493 N.W.2d 551, 553 (Minn. 1992).

3. *In re* Gustafson, 493 N.W.2d 551, 553–54 (Minn. 1992); for contrary rule, *see e.g.,* Washington, D.C., Rules of Professional Conduct, Rule 1.15(d).

4. *See supra* note 3.

5. MODEL CODE DR 2-110(A)(3); MODEL RULES Rule 1.16(d).

6. Rule 1.15, MODEL RULES; *In re* Biggs, 864 P.2d 1310, 1316, 318 Or. 281 (Or. 1994); *see also supra* note 3.

7. In New York, nonrefundable retainers are prohibited. *In re* Cooperman, 611 N.Y.S.2d 465, 83 N.Y.2d 465, 633 N.E.2d 1069 (N.Y. 1994).

8. *In re* Biggs, 864 P.2d 1310, 1316, 318 Or. 281 (Or. 1994); *contra In re* Gustafson, 493 N.W.2d 551, 553 (Minn. 1992), holding that a nonrefundable fee is earned when received; New Hampshire State Bar Formal Ethics Op. 1990-91/10 (April 11, 1991).

9. Louisiana v. Kilgarlin, 550 So. 2d 600, 604–05 (La. 1989); *contra In re* Jackson, 867 P.2d 278, 280, 254 Kan. 406 (Kan. 1994).

10. Louisiana v. Kilgarlin, 550 So. 2d 600, 604–05 (La. 1989); *contra* Oregon State Bar Legal Ethics Comm. Op. 509 (Oct. 1986), where a fixed fee in criminal case is nonrefundable, it must go into general account.

## Handling Client Costs

1. MODEL RULES at 258; Louisiana State Bar Ass'n v. Williams, 512 So. 2d 404, *reh'g denied* (La. 1987); *contra* MODEL CODE DR 9-102(A).

2. Louisiana State Bar Ass'n v. Williams, 512 So. 2d 404, *reh'g denied* (La. 1987).

3. North Carolina State Bar Ass'n Ethics Comm. Op. 51.

## Dealing with Excess and Unexplained Funds

1. Idaho State Bar Ass'n Formal Op. 122; Maryland State Bar Ass'n Formal Op. 87-18; North Carolina RPC-149.

2. Michigan State Bar Ethics Op. RI-222 (Oct. 21, 1992); Nebraska State Bar Ass'n Ethics Op. No. 93-3.

3. Rhode Island State Bar Formal Op. No. 93-19 (April 21, 1993).

4. Idaho State Bar Ass'n Formal Op. 122; Maryland State Bar Ass'n Formal Op. 87-18; North Carolina RPC-149; South Carolina State Bar Ethics Op. No. 95-3.

### Dealing with Shortages

1. Guzzetta v. State Bar, 43 Cal. 3d 962, 978–79 (Cal. 1987).
2. *See supra,* citations within "A Lawyer Can Be Disciplined Even If No One Is Hurt."
3. *In re* Respondent E, 1 State Bar Cal. Rptr. 716 (Cal. Rev. Dep't 1991).
4. MODEL RULES at 257–58.

### What to Do with Disputed Amounts

1. *In re* Cacioppo, 2 Cal. State Bar Ct. Rptr. 128, 146 (Cal. State Bar Ct. Review Dep't 1992).
2. MODEL RULES Rule 1.15(c); MODEL CODE DR 9-102(A).
3. *See, e.g.,* CAL. BUS. & PROF. CODE §§ 6200 et seq.

## PART III
## AVOIDING DISPUTES OVER TRUST ACCOUNTS

### Avoiding Disputes

1. *In re* Cacioppo, 2 Cal. State Bar Ct. Rptr. 128, 146 (Cal. State Bar Ct. Review Dep't 1992).
2. *In re* Bancroft, 505 A.2d 967, 102 N.J. 114 (N.J. 1986).
3. Michigan State Bar Ass'n Ethics Op. No. RI-222.
4. A lawyer may transfer funds for payment of attorney's fees after giving written notice to the client and receiving written consent from the client. Illinois State Bar Ass'n Comm. on Professional Ethics Op. 88-15 (May 10, 1989).

### Notifying and Accounting to the Client

1. MODEL RULES Rule 1.15(b); MODEL CODE DR 9-102(B)(1).
2. Both ABA Model Rules require prompt notification.
3. The California Supreme Court found that a lawyer was culpable of violating this rule when the lawyer failed to notify the client after three weeks of receipt of funds and failed to notify the client of the exact amount of the settlement. McKnight v. State Bar (1991) 53 Cal. 3d 1025, 1029, 1031–33; *see also* Silver v. State Bar (1974) 13 Cal. 3d 134, 143–45, disapproving a hiatus of one month between receipt and notification.
4. MODEL RULES Rule 1.15(b); MODEL CODE DR 9-102(B)(3); *In re* Wade, 814 P.2d 753 (Ariz. 1991).
5. In *In re* Hedges, 836 P.2d 119, 313 Or. 618 (Or. 1992), the Oregon Supreme Court held that an accounting regarding a personal injury settlement given fourteen months after disbursements were made was not a

prompt accounting. *See also* CAL. BUS. & PROF. CODE § 6148(b), which describes the obligation to bill the client within thirty-one days of each prior billing and Trust Accounting Standards adopted pursuant to Rule 4-100(C), Rules of Professional Conduct of the State Bar of California.

## The Duty to Pay the Client

1. MODEL RULES Rule 1.15(b). Exceptions: except as stated in Rule 1.15, as otherwise provided by law or by agreement with the client. MODEL CODE DR 9-102(B)(4). Note: The duty to pay out funds is at the request of the client and when the client is entitled to receive the funds.

2. MODEL RULES Rule 1.16(d). The rule sets no time for refund but the lawyer must take steps to the extent reasonably practicable to protect the client's interests. MODEL CODE DR 2-110(A)(3) requires promptness in the return of unearned fees.

3. But, since MODEL RULES Rule 1.16(d) requires the lawyer must take steps to the extent reasonably practicable to protect the client's interests, there may be a greater need to move quickly for the financially needy client.

4. MODEL RULES Rule 1.15, cmt., para. 2. *See also* MODEL CODE DR 9-102(A)(2).

5. MODEL RULES Rule 1.15(b) and MODEL CODE DR 9-102(B)(4) and (A)(2). Model Rules at 262. *In re* Respondent E (Review Dep't 1991) 1 Cal. State Bar Ct. Rptr. 716.

6. MODEL RULES Rule 1.5, cmt., "Disputes Over Fees." *See, e.g.,* CAL. BUS. & PROF. CODE §§ 6200 et seq. Note: Los Angeles County Bar Ass'n Op. No. 309 (March 20, 1969) opines that there is no duty to initiate a fee arbitration under law.

7. MODEL RULES Rule 1.15(b). MODEL CODE DR 9-102(B)(4).

8. MODEL RULES Rule 1.15(b), cmt., paras. 2–3.

9. What is prompt? Where lawyer had no proof of a medical lien by a medical provider, delay of one month in paying out funds was not unreasonable. *In re* Riley (Review Dep't 1994) 3 Cal. State Bar Ct. Rptr. 91. Failure to disburse proceeds for over three years is too long. *In re* Draper, 317 A.2d 106 (Del. 1974).

## The Commingling Prohibition

1. MODEL RULES Rule 1.15(a). MODEL CODE DR 9-102(A).

2. MODEL RULES Rule 1.15(c) and cmt. thereto at para. 1. MODEL CODE DR 9-102(A).

3. MODEL CODE DR 9-102(A)(2).

4. *In re* Ortega, 688 P.2d 329, 331 (N.M. 1984), disciplined a lawyer for using trust accounts to shelter funds from the IRS.

5. North Carolina State Bar v. Speckman, 87 N.C. App. 116, 360 S.E.2d 129 (1987).

6. MODEL RULES Rule 1.15(b)(c) and cmt., para. 2. MODEL CODE DR 9-102(A)(2).

7. *In re* Fonte (Review Dep't 1993) 2 Cal. State Bar Ct. Rptr. 752.

8. MODEL RULES Rule 1.15; MODEL RULES at 252. The exception in MODEL CODE DR 9-102(A)(2) was not included in Rule 1.15. But some states are permitting via ethics opinions.

9. MODEL CODE DR 9-102(A)(1). Note that this exception is no longer permitted. *See supra* note 7.

10. Columbus Bar Ass'n v. Thompson, 69 Ohio St. 2d 667, 433 N.E.2d 602 (1982).

11. MODEL CODE DR 9-102(A)(2).

12. Title 22, New York Codes, Rules & Regulations, § 1200.46(b)(1) [DR 9-102] New York Code of Professional Responsibility.

## Nonclient and Third-Party Claims

1. MODEL RULES Rule 1.15.

2. ABA/BNA MANUAL at 45:1203.

3. Contractual liens: *see In re* Riley (Review Dep't 1994) 3 Cal. State Bar Ct. Rptr. 91.

4. Statutory liens: *see In re* Respondent P, 2 Cal. State Bar Ct. Rptr. 622, 627, 630 (1993 Cal. State Bar Ct. Rev. Dep't).

5. Connecticut Bar Ass'n Comm. on Professional Ethics Op. No. 92-5 (Jan. 27, 1992).

6. ABA/BNA MANUAL at 45:1203–04.

7. North Carolina State Bar Ass'n Legal Ethics Comm. Op. No. 75; Alabama State Bar Op. 388 and 86-63 (July 10, 1986).

8. *See* Rhode Island State Bar Op. No. 93-19 (April 21, 1993), opining that a lawyer may continue to hold a client's money in a client trust account as long as holding such funds is not for the purpose of defrauding any third party.

9. Virginia State Bar Standing Comm. on Legal Ethics Op. No. 1579 (April 11, 1994).

## The Offense of Misappropriation

1. *See* State *ex rel.* Oklahoma State Bar Ass'n v. Dunlap, 880 P.2d 364, 367 (Okla. 1994); ABA/BNA MANUAL at 45:501–02.

2. ABA/BNA MANUAL at. 45:502.

3. ABA/BNA MANUAL at 45:503.

4. ABA/BNA MANUAL at 45:503.

5. Florida Bar v. Solomon, 589 So. 2d 286 (Fla. 1991); *In re* Moras, 619 A.2d 1007, 1010–11, 131 N.J. 164 (N.J. 1993) (advancing funds from clients' trust account to accommodate clients where the draft or check has not yet cleared; Exception: real estate or commercial closings).

### Endorsing Clients' Names on Checks

1. *In re* Lazarus (Review Dep't 1991) 1 Cal. State Bar Ct. Rptr. 387, 393, 395; ABA/BNA MANUAL at 45:511.
2. *In re* Lazarus (Review Dep't 1991) 1 Cal. State Bar Ct. Rptr. 387, 393, 395.
3. *See, e.g.,* Palomo v. State Bar (1984) 36 Cal. 3d 785, 793–95. However, in some circumstances a lawyer may sign a release (e.g., when the lawyer has an express special power of attorney). *See In re* Lazarus (Review Dep't 1991) 1 Cal. State Bar Ct. Rptr. 387.

### Currency Transactions Involving the Trust Account

1. *See, e.g.,* 26 U.S.C. § 60501.
2. MODEL RULES Rule 1.15; MODEL CODE DR 9-102(A).
3. *See, e.g.,* 26 U.S.C. § 60501.

### Withheld Payroll Taxes

1. *In re* Morales, 35 Cal. 3d 1, 196 Cal. Rptr. 353 (Cal. 1983).
2. New Jersey Advisory Comm. on Professional Ethics Op. No. 598 (March 26, 1987).
3. New Jersey Advisory Comm. on Professional Ethics Op. No. 598 (March 26, 1987).

## PART IV
## DEALING WITH SPECIAL TRUST ACCOUNT PROBLEMS

### Ethical Problems Caused by Service of Process

1. *See, e.g.,* CAL. EVID. CODE § 958; CAL. CIV. PROC. CODE § 2018(e).
2. Connecticut State Bar Op. 92-28; *see also* South Carolina State Bar Op. 92-35.
3. Connecticut State Bar Op. 92-28; *see also* South Carolina State Bar Op. 92-35.

### The Dishonored Trust Account Deposit Trap

1. One insufficiently funded check drawn on the trust account, coupled with the lawyer's repeated, unkept promises to make good on the check, and failing to make good on it, can constitute moral turpitude within

the meaning of Bus. & Prof. Code § 6106. Bowles v. State Bar, 48 Cal. 3d 100, 104–05, 109 (1989). However, mere failure to keep a promise is not evidence of fraudulent intent. *In re* Mapps, 1 Cal. State Bar Ct. Rptr. 1, 12 (Cal. State Bar Ct. Review Dep't 1990).

2. Florida Bar v. Solomon, 589 So. 2d 286 (Fla. 1991); *In re* Moras, 619 A.2d 1007, 1010–11, 131 N.J. 164 (N.J. 1993) (advancing funds from clients' trust account to accommodate clients where the draft or check has not yet cleared; Exception: real estate or commercial closings).

## Handling "Rush-Rush" Settlements

1. Florida Bar v. Solomon, 589 So. 2d 286 (Fla. 1991); *In re* Moras, 619 A.2d 1007, 1010–11, 131 N.J. 164 (N.J. 1993) (advancing funds from clients' trust account to accommodate clients where the draft or check has not yet cleared; Exception: real estate or commercial closings).

## Getting the Fee as Quickly as Possible

1. *In re* Lazarus (Review Dep't 1991) 1 Cal. State Bar Ct. Rptr. 387.

2. *See, e.g.,* Palomo v. State Bar (1984), 36 Cal. 3d 785, 794; Silver v. State Bar (1974), 13 Cal. 3d 134, 144; Montalto v. State Bar (1974), 11 Cal. 3d 231, 235; Himmel v. State Bar (1971), 4 Cal. 3d 786, 798.

3. Assuming that a lawyer has a written special power of attorney, a lawyer may not lead a third party to believe that the client had personally signed a document, where the third party desires the actual endorsement of the client and where the lawyer signed the document under an express agreement with the client. *See* Hallinan v. State Bar (1948), 33 Cal. 2d 246, 249; Levin v. State Bar (1989), 47 Cal. 3d 1140, 1146.

## Out of Trust = In Trouble

1. Reeck v. Polk, 257 N.W.2d 698, 699, 269 Mich. 262 (Mich. 1934); *In re* Tidball, 503 N.W.2d 850 (S.D. 1993).

2. *In re* Galbasini, 163 Ariz. 120, 124; 786 P.2d 971, 975 (Ariz. 1990).

3. *In re* Respondent E, 1 Cal. State Bar Ct. Rptr. 716 (Cal. State Bar Ct. Review Dep't 1991).

## Using a Backup Line of Credit

1. *See, e.g.,* Cal. Bus. & Prof. Code §§ 6091.1(a) and (b)(2).

2. Reeck v. Polk, 257 N.W.2d 698, 699, 269 Mich. 262 (Mich. 1934); *In re* Tidball, 503 N.W.2d 850 (S.D. 1993).

## PART V
## KEEPING TRUST ACCOUNT RECORDS

### Segregate and Distinguish Client Trust Account Records and Checks from Other Records and Checks

1. *In re* Lamb, 585 A.2d 326, 327 (N.J. 1991) (failure to produce records after audit request); *see also* MODEL RULES at 260.

2. *See, e.g.,* Rule 4-100(B)(3), Rules of Professional Conduct of the State Bar of California (requiring preservation of records for five years after "final appropriate distribution" of the funds).

### Common Trust Account Records and Documents

1. ABA MODEL RECORD KEEPING RULE; Title 22, New York Codes, Rules & Regulations, § 1200.46(d) [DR 9-102(d)] New York Code of Professional Responsibility.

2. Standard 1(a) to Rule 4-100 (C), California Rules of Professional Conduct.

3. *See, e.g.,* Rule 4-100(C) and standards promulgated thereunder; STATE BAR OF CALIFORNIA, HANDBOOK ON CLIENT TRUST ACCOUNTING FOR CALIFORNIA ATTORNEYS, at 18–19 (November 1992).

### Special Trust Account Terms

1. *See, e.g.,* Standard (1)(b), Trust Account Record Keeping Standard adopted under Rule 4-100(C), Rules of Professional Conduct of the State Bar of California; *see also* DR 9-102(D), New York Rules of Professional Conduct.

2. *See, e.g.,* Standard (1)(a), Trust Account Record Keeping Standard adopted under Rule 4-100(C), Rules of Professional Conduct of the State Bar of California.

3. *See, e.g.,* DR 9-102(D), (H), New York Rules of Professional Conduct.

4. *See, e.g.,* Standard (1)(d), Trust Account Record Keeping Standard adopted under Rule 4-100(C), Rules of Professional Conduct of the State Bar of California.

# APPENDIX A

## WHERE TO GET HELP

From time to time a lawyer needs help making a decision. The mere fact that the lawyer called for help may be important if a mistake is made and there is a subsequent question of negligence or willfulness in making the mistake. The calls the lawyer makes and the lawyer's reliance on the answers given may save a license in an appropriate situation.

The following is a list of people or institutions that may be willing to help a lawyer with a question concerning trust accounts and trust account maintenance. It is strongly recommended that the reader immediately research and fill in the fax and phone numbers for the sources listed onto the following pages. Record the information using the "Trust Account Help List" provided at the end of this appendix. Keep the list readily available. In addition, copy the information into your computer or personal information manager.

Not all of the listed sources are available in every state. Some homework will have to be done to fill in the telephone numbers for the listed sources. Some of the listed sources may only give specific answers to specific questions. In some cases only references to the appropriate rules can be gotten. In most cases the advice will be free by telephone or electronic mail, but there may be a charge if there is extensive research done or if copies of cases or opinions are to be mailed or faxed to you. In almost every case, the help given will not be legally binding on anyone, due to lack of time to get all the applicable facts.

If calls are made to these sources for help, you should make and retain a hard-copy record of the call, including the number called, the person with whom you spoke, and the help given or not given. Do not rely on a computer record as there often is no statute of limitations for ethics complaints and it may not be possible to read the computer records years later when the system is obsolete.

Telephone bills can substantiate written records. For 800 numbers the caller may have no record of the call, as the called number will get the bill. When there is a choice between the 800 number and a long-distance or local number, use the long-distance or local number to create a record in your possession and control should you need it years later. Records of the 800 number called may be able to show the date, time, and phone from which the call was made. You can obtain 800 numbers through 1 (800) 555-1212.

A few comments describing each source of help have been added. These comments are generally accurate, but may or may not be accurate for a given listed source in a given jurisdiction.

It is strongly recommended that the homework be done before help is needed. Many of the telephone numbers are not easy to find. Often one must attempt several wrong numbers to find the right number. In some cases the only number available will be the offices of the bar, typically in or near the state capitol. There may or may not be an 800 number or a local number to call. It will take some time and calling around to get the information and immediate help may be needed. Fill in the numbers as soon as possible. Fax and U.S. mail and electronic mail should all be used to create a record if one can't get through on the telephone outside of normal business hours or because of busy signals on the telephone.

**1. State Bar Ethics Hot Line.** Most mandatory state bars and most voluntary bar associations have some form of an ethics hot line available to members during normal office hours. The number is typically an 800 number, but often not listed in the 800 directory.

Unfortunately the quality and responsiveness of the help you get varies greatly from state to state. In some states you will get immediate help from a competent lawyer. In some states you will get to leave your name and number on a voice mail system and may or may not get a call back in a few minutes, a few hours, or a few weeks. In some states you will get an inexperienced law student who is getting paid minimum wage or no wage. The student may know more or less than you about the question you are asking.

Some of the organizations will give you specific answers to your questions, and some will only suggest that you read certain cases or opinions that seem to be on point based on your statement of the facts and the question.

If you ever become a bar leader, I ask you to work toward improving the level of this service in your jurisdiction. We are dealing with public trust and confidence in the system, we are dealing with the public's money, and we are dealing with your license to practice law. It is beyond me why the organization to which you pay dues will spend hundreds of dollars per lawyer per year of your money to prosecute ethics violators, but won't spend pennies to help prevent ethics violations by offering help to the people who pay the dues. (This is an editorial comment).

**2. Local Bar Association(s) Ethics Hot Line.** Your county bar and city bar and specialty bar may have an ethics hot line.

**3. American Bar Association.** The ABA in Chicago has an ethics hot line available to both members and nonmembers. Telephone help is normally free, but there will be a charge for anything more (with different prices for members and nonmembers). You may have to call the ABA on a long-distance basis because it does not have an 800 number.

**4. IOLTA.** Your IOLTA office may be able to answer your question by telephone or point you in the right direction. IOLTA people are usually very knowledgeable about applicable trust account rules and regulations, but are sometimes unwilling or unable to help you due to self-imposed or statutorily imposed restrictions on their activities.

**5. State and Local Bar Ethics Committee Members.** Most lawyers will help another lawyer when help is needed. The members of your ethics committee will normally try to give you some limited help or point you in the right direction to get help. In some cases the committee will only help government agencies or respond to formal requests made by the board of directors of the organization, but the individual lawyer may at least give you some phone numbers to call.

**6. Bar General Counsel.** Don't confuse bar general counsel with bar disciplinary counsel. In most (not all) cases they will be two totally different offices with totally different staff and very different functions. In some states the office of the bar general counsel will help a lawyer with a trust account or other ethics question. In some states they won't help you but may point you in the right direction.

As might be expected from the title, the bar general counsel is the in-house lawyer for the bar. They sometimes, but not usually, prosecute ethics and trust account violations.

**7. Bar Disciplinary Counsel.** Bar disciplinary counsel are the lawyers who prosecute trust account violations. They normally are rather "prosecution minded" and won't respond to requests for help because of a concern that their good faith attempts to help you may in some manner contaminate a later prosecution if required. In some cases they might help you or at least point you in the right direction to get help.

**8. Your Malpractice Insurance Carrier.** Your malpractice insurance carrier may be called upon to defend you or to pay indemnity if there is a trust account violation claim against you. Accordingly, many malpractice carriers have expertise in trust account management. Unfortunately, your call to them may result in you being placed in a higher risk category when they open a file on your inquiry or they may send you a bill claiming that the cost of assisting you must be paid by you as part of your deductible. You may try to call them on an anonymous basis.

**9. Your Bar Law Office Management Advisory Service.** I personally have worked for many years to try to get state bars to install practice management advisors to help lawyers with management questions, including trust account management questions. The oldest and most experienced law office management advisory service is the Florida Bar Law Office Management Advisory Service created in 1981 and continually directed since that time by J. R. Phelps. The second oldest is the Oregon Bar service created in 1983 and directed continuously since that time by Carol Wilson. Other states began installing programs in 1992 when the New York State Bar Association created an office under Steve Gallagher. Other states have recently begun installing programs. Some of these newer programs are run by insurance companies and may or may not help noninsureds. A call to either the Florida Bar in Tallahassee or the Oregon Bar in Lake Oswego or the New York State Bar Association in Albany may help you determine if such an advisor exists in your state and how to access the office.

**10. Your CPA.** Your CPA will be of great help in installing an accounting system for your trust account and in reconciling the bank and ledger balances of the trust accounts. Unfortunately, the CPA may have little or no understanding of what a lawyer's trust account is and what ethical issues are involved. Your CPA will be necessary to maintain the proper records, but don't depend solely on the CPA to answer an ethics question even if you are confident the CPA really knows legal ethics.

**11. Professional Responsibility Lawyers.** Lawyers who specialize or assist in defending lawyers accused of ethics violations call themselves professional responsibility lawyers. They have an organization called the Association of Professional Responsibility Lawyers (known by the acronym APRL). I belong to that organization, which is affiliated with the ABA in Chicago. The ABA office in Chicago that assists APRL may be able to give you the name(s) of lawyers in your area who may be able to help.

**12. Ethics Mentor.** Every lawyer should have a network of mentors with whom difficult problems can be discussed and who can act both as a sounding board and a suggestion source. You should have such a mentor in the ethics area as well as in other substantive law areas.

Following is a blank "Trust Account Help List" into which you can insert phone numbers, fax numbers, e-mail numbers, addresses, etc. You should get the information for this list as soon as you can, *before* you need it.

Following the phone number list are two blank pages for you to use to record your attempts to get help. You may need this written record to establish your bona fide attempts to comply with trust account requirements. By keeping the record in this trust account manual, you'll always know where to find your record.

# TRUST ACCOUNT HELP LIST

City(s) and state(s) in which you practice or intend to practice:

_____

_____

_____

_____

| Agency | Telephone | Fax | E-mail | U.S. Mail |
|---|---|---|---|---|
| State Bar Ethics Hot Line | | | | |
| Local Bar Association Ethics Hot Line | | | | |
| ABA Ethics Hot Line | | | | |
| IOLTA—Interest on Lawyer Trust Accounts | | | | |
| State and Local Bar Ethics Committee Chairs or Members | | | | |
| Bar General Counsel | | | | |
| Bar Disciplinary Counsel | | | | |
| Malpractice Insurance Carrier | | | | |
| Bar Law Office Management Advisory Service | | | | |
| Your CPA | | | | |
| Association of Professional Responsibility Lawyers | | | | |

| Agency | Telephone | Fax | E-mail | U.S. Mail |
|---|---|---|---|---|
| Where to Get a Copy of Current Rules | | | | |
| Ethics Mentor (s) | | | | |
| Other | | | | |

DO NOT REMOVE THESE PAGES FROM THIS BOOK.
A RECORD OF CONTACTS MADE MAY BE NECESSARY
AT A LATER TIME.

## RECORD OF CONTACTS TO SEEK HELP
## ON TRUST ACCOUNT QUESTION(S)

Indicate telephone number(s) called, agency(s) called, person(s) with whom you spoke or left message(s), time and date of contact(s), question phrased, and answer given. Indicate whether call or contact was outgoing or incoming (for evidentiary purposes if necessary). Indicate if you have or will prepare additional written dictated records of your contacts to seek help. Keep all telephone bills to document contacts.

Include as much information as possible, including date, number called, agency called, person contacted, message left, questions asked, answers or advice given, and other comments.

1. _____
_____
_____
_____

2. _____
_____
_____
_____

3. _____
_____
_____
_____

4. _____
_____
_____
_____

5. _____
_____
_____
_____

6. _____
_____
_____
_____

7._____
_____
_____
_____
_____

8._____
_____
_____
_____

9. _____
_____
_____
_____

10._____
_____
_____
_____

11. _____
_____
_____
_____

12. _____
_____
_____
_____

13. _____
_____
_____
_____

14. _____
_____
_____
_____

# APPENDIX B

## TRUST ACCOUNT SELF-TEST

The following test is based on the materials contained in this book. The materials are based on a lawyer's common-law and statutory ethical duties as contained in the American Bar Association Canons of Professional Ethics, the ABA Code of Professional Conduct, the ABA Model Rules of Professional Conduct, and the more recent IOLTA rules.

The test is designed to test recognition of the most common issues a practicing lawyer will have to deal with in the practice of law. It is presumed that if the lawyer can recognize the issues, the lawyer can seek help in getting advice based on interpretations that reflect current interpretations in a particular jurisdiction.

Knowledge of trust account terminology and procedures as contained in the materials is tested, but the test is not intended as an applied bookkeeping skills demonstration.

The issues presented in the materials and the test have not been tested in all jurisdictions, and there will be differences from time to time in local interpretation. Additionally, positions of disciplinary authorities can and do change, often 180 degrees. Accordingly, recognition of the issues is tested rather than specific knowledge of a given state's disciplinary or IOLTA rules.

### To Course Instructors

If specific recognition of a specific state's rules is to be tested, it is recommended that a supplemental short test be prepared with specific questions to augment specific questions in this test.

A third column is provided to block out questions that are not to be answered.

**TRUE  FALSE OMIT**

1. Basic trust account principles are found in the common law of fiduciary and beneficiary.

TRUE     FALSE     OMIT

2. The prohibition against commingling client trust funds and attorney funds is found in the 1909 American Bar Association Canons of Ethics, the 1970 American Bar Association's Model Code of Professional Responsibility, and the 1983 American Bar Association's Model Code of Professional Conduct.

TRUE     FALSE     OMIT

3. The requirement that a lawyer promptly notify a client of receipt of funds belonging to the client can be found in the 1909 American Bar Association's Canons of Ethics, the 1970 American Bar Association's Model Code of Professional Responsibility, and the 1983 American Bar Association's Model Code of Professional Conduct.

TRUE     FALSE     OMIT

4. The American Bar Association's 1909 Canons of Ethics was copied from the Alabama Bar Association's Code of Ethics, which itself was fashioned in 1887 on works published in 1836 and 1850.

TRUE     FALSE     OMIT

5. In the event of a conflict between state bar rules and ABA principles, the ABA principles are controlling.

TRUE     FALSE     OMIT

6. IOLTA is an acronym for Interest on Lawyers' Trust Accounts.

TRUE     FALSE     OMIT

7. IOLTA was created by the American Bar Association in the 1983 Model Code of Professional Responsibility.

TRUE     FALSE     OMIT

8. Trust account violations are governed by the "no harm, no foul rule." A lawyer cannot be disciplined if the clients eventually get their money.

TRUE    FALSE    OMIT

9. An intervening third-party criminal act, such as a bookkeeper embezzling funds, relieves the lawyer of financial responsibility for trust account monies.

TRUE    FALSE    OMIT

10. An intervening third-party criminal act, such as a bookkeeper embezzling funds, relieves the lawyer of disciplinary responsibility.

TRUE    FALSE    OMIT

11. Attorney-client trust account terminology is the same as the terminology used in generally accepted commercial accounting.

TRUE    FALSE    OMIT

12. Attorney-client trust account reports are the same reports with the same terminology as one would find in normal commercial accounting reports.

TRUE    FALSE    OMIT

13. It is permissible for the lawyer's fees to remain in the trust account after they are earned as long as the clients timely get their money.

TRUE    FALSE    OMIT

14. Using rubber-stamp signatures for trust account checks is a preferred trust account procedure because it saves the lawyer the time and bother of reviewing disbursements before checks are signed.

TRUE    FALSE    OMIT

15. Using mechanical or computer-generated or preprinted signatures for the trust account checks is a recommended procedure because it is efficient and saves the lawyer the bother of reviewing the disbursements before signing the checks.

TRUE    FALSE    OMIT

16. Unearned fees the lawyer expects to earn in the month received can be placed in the office account before the fee is earned.

TRUE    FALSE    OMIT

17. The term "retainer fee" has different meanings in different jurisdictions and in different situations, resulting in differing rules as to whether or not a "retainer fee" must or must not be deposited to the trust account.

TRUE    FALSE    OMIT

18. "Retainer fees" can be deposited to the office account if the retainer fee is earned in full by the act of accepting the client or matter and is not refundable.

TRUE    FALSE    OMIT

19. "Retainer fees" that are in fact advanced deposits on fees to be earned must be deposited to the trust account.

TRUE    FALSE    OMIT

20. It is permissible to use a general office account as a trust account as long as no client loses money.

TRUE    FALSE    OMIT

21. Paying annual bar dues with a trust account check is aggressive stupidity.

TRUE    FALSE    OMIT

22. An insurance company draft is as good as cash and a lawyer can safely issue checks to the client and to third parties and for fees and costs the moment the draft is listed on the deposit ticket and delivered to the bank.

TRUE    FALSE    OMIT

23. Cashier's checks and bank money orders are as good as cash and a lawyer can safely immediately issue trust account checks against the deposit of a cashier's check or bank money order without waiting for the check to clear the drawee bank.

TRUE    FALSE    OMIT

24. When a lawyer receives a settlement draft or check with permission to deposit the check upon execution of a document, it is permissible to deposit the check and distribute

the proceeds before getting the required signatures on the document in order to save time.

TRUE    FALSE    OMIT

25. A lawyer may endorse a client's signature to a settlement check or draft if the lawyer has appropriate written authority to do so, but a lawyer should not execute a settlement agreement by signing a client's signature if it can be avoided.

TRUE    FALSE    OMIT

26. A check certified by a bank (a certified check) is normally as good as cash.

TRUE    FALSE    OMIT

27. Generally, all unearned fees must be placed in the trust account until earned.

TRUE    FALSE    OMIT

28. Generally, unearned fees in the trust account belong to the client and are subject to the client's creditors, tax liens, bankruptcy trustee, etc.

TRUE    FALSE    OMIT

29. A lawyer generally may ethically provide for a lien on the client's cause of action or recovery or funds in the trust account to protect the lawyer from third-party claims.

TRUE    FALSE    OMIT

30. A lawyer can delegate trust account responsibility to a professional office manager or licensed Certified Public Accountant and not be disciplined for trust account mistakes made by the paralegal or the office manager.

TRUE    FALSE    OMIT

31. A lawyer can delegate trust account responsibility to a professional office manager or licensed CPA and have no financial responsibility for mistakes made by the paralegal or office manager.

TRUE    FALSE    OMIT

32. In a large firm with a managing partner and a chief financial officer and an in-house CPA, a lawyer will still have personal disciplinary responsibility or financial responsibil-

ity for trust account negligence, mistakes, and irregularities on those cases under the lawyer's control or supervision.

TRUE    FALSE    OMIT

33. In large firms it is an acceptable practice for each lawyer who has case responsibility to have his or her own client trust account in addition to the firm's client trust account.

TRUE    FALSE    OMIT

34. It is permissible for a lawyer to "borrow" funds from the trust account for short periods of time as long as the clients get their money in a reasonably prompt time.

TRUE    FALSE    OMIT

35. A lawyer may remove fees as earned from a client trust account without prior approval as to the amount of the fees if the fee agreement with the client so provides.

TRUE    FALSE    OMIT

36. If a lawyer removes earned fees from a client trust account in accordance with the fee agreement, and the client subsequently objects to the amount of the fees, the lawyer must immediately return the fees to the trust account until the dispute is resolved.

TRUE    FALSE    OMIT

37. A lawyer who keeps trust account records in a computer can be disciplined for failure to keep proper records if the computer crashes and no monthly hard copies were prepared.

TRUE    FALSE    OMIT

38. It is a good practice to delay opening a trust bank account until the lawyer actually has client funds that need depositing to a trust account.

TRUE    FALSE    OMIT

39. Under most IOLTA rules, a bank is not required to report a bounced trust account check to the bar or to IOLTA if the lawyer makes good on the check out of personal funds in a reasonable time and the trust account check clears the second time it is deposited.

TRUE    FALSE    OMIT

40. In some states an auditor will audit all transactions on a trust account for three years, even if the bank bounced a check through a bank computer error and the lawyer did nothing wrong.

TRUE    FALSE    OMIT

41. Only client funds have to go into the trust account. Funds paid by one nonclient to another nonclient incident to representation of a client can be deposited to the office account or to an interest-bearing account with interest going to the lawyer.

TRUE    FALSE    OMIT

42. If the client's money or a third party's money is likely to be with the lawyer long enough to earn significant interest, the lawyer should not put the money into an IOLTA account, but rather should open a special trust account whereby the interest can be credited or given to the person ultimately entitled to the interest.

TRUE    FALSE    OMIT

43. The interest earned on IOLTA accounts is normally used for a "charitable" purpose such as legal aid or poverty law or other law-related assistance to the poor.

TRUE    FALSE    OMIT

44. A law firm may properly combine cash in the client trust account with the cash in its other bank accounts on the financial statements of the firm as long as an appropriate footnote is included in the financial statements.

TRUE    FALSE    OMIT

45. A bank may stop payment on its cashier's check if requested to do so by the customer who purchased the check.

TRUE    FALSE    OMIT

46. If a client wire transfers funds to a lawyer's trust account and asks the lawyer to turn the funds into cash for delivery to a political campaign, the lawyer need not be concerned over civil or criminal implications because the lawyer is obligated to follow a client's instruction as to trust accounts and it is not the duty of a lawyer to police the client's affairs.

TRUE    FALSE    OMIT

47. Assume a client gives a law firm a check with instructions to deposit the check to the trust account and await further instructions. The client subsequently instructs the lawyer to send a series of checks for $950 each to a political campaign fund and to identify the source of the funds as "anonymous." The lawyer knows (or should know) that it is a violation of state election law for one person to donate more than $1,000 to a single campaign fund. Possible violation of the election law is of concern to the client and is no concern of the lawyer.

TRUE    FALSE    OMIT

48. A client asks a lawyer to bill the client's company "for services rendered" with no further description and to put the payment into the trust account to await further instructions. The lawyer need not be concerned with the client's tax treatment of the payment of the invoice as deductibility or nondeductibility of the payment by the company is the concern of the client and not of the lawyer.

TRUE    FALSE    OMIT

49. A client who is the president of a corporation asks the lawyer to invoice the corporation "for services rendered" and to deposit the payment to the trust account and await further instructions. The lawyer has no ethical duties to the corporation. That is a matter between the corporation and its president.

TRUE    FALSE    OMIT

50. A lawyer may deposit funds received for services previously rendered into the trust account if the lawyer reasonably believes there will be a dispute over the fees.

TRUE    FALSE    OMIT

51. After reconciling the trust account bank statement to the trust account records and being satisfied that all balances are correct, the lawyer may then trash the reconciliation and supporting data used to make the reconciliation.

TRUE    FALSE    OMIT

52. On receipt of service of process seeking financial information (including information from or concerning the trust ac-

count), the lawyer must assert all reasonably assertable privileges to protect all clients' identities and legal matters.

TRUE     FALSE     OMIT

53. On receipt of service of process seeking financial information (including financial information concerning or from the trust account), the lawyer should notify all clients whose financial and legal affairs would be disclosed to third parties to determine if the clients wish to assert appropriate privileges.

TRUE     FALSE     OMIT

54. On receipt of process to obtain information from a client's trust account, a lawyer should consider taking appropriate action to seek judicial review of the process and a protective or limiting order to protect clients' confidences.

TRUE     FALSE     OMIT

55. The attorney-client privilege and protection of client confidences normally cannot be maintained by a lawyer when the lawyer's own affairs are the subject of a disciplinary agency inquiry.

TRUE     FALSE     OMIT

56. Attorney-client privilege and confidences should be maintained for clients whose affairs are not the subject of inquiry.

TRUE     FALSE     OMIT

57. Whether or not it is required, it is good practice to physically segregate client trust account bank statements, cancelled checks, reconciliations, and other documents from other banking records.

TRUE     FALSE     OMIT

58. A lawyer has satisfied ethical trust account obligations by delegating trust account maintenance to a CPA and then not being further involved except to sign trust account checks prepared by the CPA.

TRUE     FALSE     OMIT

59. When a client notifies a lawyer of an assignment of funds in the trust account to a third party, and subsequently in-

structs the lawyer to disregard the assignment, the lawyer has no ethical responsibility to honor the assignment or to hold onto the funds until the dispute is resolved.

TRUE    FALSE    OMIT

60. It is ethically permissible to contract with a client to charge the client for the performance of trust account maintenance such as preparing checks, deposits, reconciliations, etc.

TRUE    FALSE    OMIT

61. A lawyer should determine if the law of interpleader or declaratory relief can provide a method for the lawyer to be relieved of maintaining trust account funds where there is a dispute.

TRUE    FALSE    OMIT

62. The term "retainer fee" has different meanings in different jurisdictions and different fact situations.

TRUE    FALSE    OMIT

63. In some states, only specifically approved institutions within the state may be used for IOLTA accounts.

TRUE    FALSE    OMIT

64. In some states, client trust accounts for the benefit of a specific client, not being subject to IOLTA, must nonetheless be maintained within the state in an approved institution.

TRUE    FALSE    OMIT

65. Under the rules in most states, a client trust account may be maintained outside the United States if for the use of a single client and the client so directs understanding there will not be insurance and there is a reasonable legitimate connection between the client's matter and the foreign jurisdiction.

TRUE    FALSE    OMIT

66. If a lawyer's trust account records are subpoenaed by disciplinary authorities, the lawyer should have copies of all records turned over in case the lawyer needs them for malpractice or tax or other purposes as the lawyer may not be able to conveniently get access to the records or copies of the records after they are delivered.

TRUE    FALSE    OMIT

67. If a lawyer chooses to maintain trust account records in a computer and the software publisher or the equipment manufacturer stops supporting the systems, the lawyer may be excused from producing records due to inability.

    TRUE    FALSE    OMIT

68. A multistate law firm may keep the client trust account and maintain the records in accordance with the laws of any state in which the firm has an office.

    TRUE    FALSE    OMIT

69. A multistate law firm should maintain a client trust account within the state where the responsible supervising lawyer for the matter is located and should follow the trust account and IOLTA rules of that state.

    TRUE    FALSE    OMIT

70. "Misappropriation" is a term commonly used to describe a variety of trust account rules violations.

    TRUE    FALSE    OMIT

71. Failure to maintain and safeguard adequate hard-copy records of computer records of trust account transactions and reconciliations can be a disciplinary offense in and of itself.

    TRUE    FALSE    OMIT

72. It is good office procedure and good law firm management to maintain separate bank accounts as follows:

    a. A client's trust account for client and third-party funds.

    TRUE    FALSE    OMIT

    b. A general office account for office expenses and to receive fee and other income.

    TRUE    FALSE    OMIT

    c. A payroll account to receive gross payrolls and to segregate withheld employee taxes.

    TRUE    FALSE    OMIT

    d. A client cost account to record client costs expended and recovered and where a "cushion" of lawyer funds belonging to the law firm may ethically be maintained.

    TRUE    FALSE    OMIT

e. A personal bank account should be maintained for the lawyer's personal nonclient-related expenditures.

TRUE    FALSE    OMIT

73. A lawyer properly opens a non-IOLTA client trust account for several clients who have an economic interest in the same large transaction. For various reasons, not the fault of the law firm, interest income belonging to one of the clients was not paid to that client and the client cannot be located or the client never cashed the check for his or her share of the interest and the lawyer wants to close the account. Since the account was not an IOLTA account, the lawyer may clear the account by a check to the firm as long as the firm pays the income tax on the interest earned.

TRUE    FALSE    OMIT

74. A lawyer who is administratively challenged and unable to balance a personal checkbook should get assistance from a CPA or part-time bookkeepers as well as get some tutoring in basic checkbook maintenance.

TRUE    FALSE    OMIT

75. When funds in the trust account have been earned by the lawyer and must be removed, the lawyer may remove them by paying personal expenses and bills directly from the client trust account without the necessity of transferring the funds directly to the office general account where the income will be reflected. Such a practice would constitute permitted commingling.

TRUE    FALSE    OMIT

76. An IOLTA bank will not report a lawyer if a trust account check is presented against insufficient funds if the lawyer covers the check before it bounces.

TRUE    FALSE    OMIT

77. The IRS claims that many lawyers underreport their income by writing checks from a trust account for personal use or personal savings without first transferring the funds to the office general account and subsequently drawing the money out for personal use.

TRUE    FALSE    OMIT

78. In some states, a lawyer must "immediately" refund un-earned legal fees to a client and must "promptly" pay to clients and third parties the funds to which they are entitled from the account.

TRUE    FALSE    OMIT

79. When a lawyer represents one party in a transaction involving trust account funds and the other party is unrepresented by a lawyer, it is wise for the lawyer when disbursing money to the nonclient to remind the nonclient in writing that the lawyer represents only his or her clients and does not represent the nonclient.

TRUE    FALSE    OMIT

80. A lawyer may deposit unearned fees or deposits to secure payment of fees directly into the office general account instead of depositing them to the client trust account if the client has knowingly given written permission to do so.

TRUE    FALSE    OMIT

81. Paying annual convention registration fees with a client trust account check is generally considered "aggressive stupidity."

TRUE    FALSE    OMIT

82. Third-party liens on settlement proceeds can be ignored if the client instructs the lawyer to pay the cash directly to the client and to leave it to the client to pay the lien amount or negotiate it down.

TRUE    FALSE    OMIT

83. A lawyer can be disciplined and held financially responsible for failure to honor contractual or statutory third-party liens on funds flowing through the trust account.

TRUE    FALSE    OMIT

84. A lawyer may safely assume that the firm's insurance policies will fully protect and cover property that is owned by the client rather than the firm.

TRUE    FALSE    OMIT

85. Lawyers who represent and defend lawyers accused of trust account violations are commonly known as professional re-

sponsibility lawyers and many can be found as members of the Association of Professional Responsibility Lawyers (APRL).

TRUE    FALSE    OMIT

86. The ABA and most state and local bar associations have some form of an ethics hot line, which may be able to assist with a trust account question.

TRUE    FALSE    OMIT

87. In many states, the IOLTA administrators may be able to assist with a trust account question.

TRUE    FALSE    OMIT

88. Malpractice insurance carriers can often assist a lawyer with a trust account question.

TRUE    FALSE    OMIT

89. In those states with law office practice management advisors, assistance can usually be gotten for trust account problems.

TRUE    FALSE    OMIT

# APPENDIX C

## ANSWERS TO TRUST ACCOUNT SELF-TEST

| | | |
|---|---|---|
| 1. True | 32. True | 63. True |
| 2. True | 33. True | 64. True |
| 3. False | 34. False | 65. True |
| 4. True | 35. True | 66. True |
| 5. False | 36. True | 67. True |
| 6. True | 37. True | 68. False |
| 7. False | 38. False | 69. True |
| 8. False | 39. False | 70. True |
| 9. False | 40. True | 71. True |
| 10. False | 41. False | 72a. True |
| 11. False | 42. True | 72b. True |
| 12. False | 43. True | 72c. True |
| 13. False | 44. False | 72d. True |
| 14. False | 45. True | 72e. True |
| 15. False | 46. False | 73. False |
| 16. False | 47. False | 74. True |
| 17. True | 48. False | 75. False |
| 18. True | 49. False | 76. False |
| 19. True | 50. False | 77. True |
| 20. False | 51. False | 78. True |
| 21. True | 52. True | 79. True |
| 22. False | 53. True | 80. False |
| 23. False | 54. True | 81. True |
| 24. False | 55. True | 82. False |
| 25. True | 56. True | 83. True |
| 26. True | 57. True | 84. False |
| 27. True | 58. False | 85. True |
| 28. True | 59. False | 86. True |
| 29. True | 60. True | 87. True |
| 30. False | 61. True | 88. True |
| 31. False | 62. True | 89. True |

# APPENDIX D

## IOLTA STAFF DIRECTORY

The American Bar Association IOLTA Clearinghouse

### ALABAMA

Ms. Tracy A. Daniel
Alabama Law Foundation Inc.
P.O. Box 671
415 Dexter Avenue
Montgomery, AL 36101
Telephone: (334) 269-1515
Fax: (334) 261-6310

### ALASKA

Ms. Deborah O'Regan
Alaska Bar Association
P.O. Box 100279
Suite 602, 510 L Street
Anchorage, AK 99510-0279
Telephone: (907) 272-7469
Fax: (907) 272-2932

### ARIZONA

Mr. Ron Johnson
Arizona Bar Foundation
Suite 1800
111 W. Monroe
Phoenix, AZ 85003-1742
Telephone: (602) 340-7372
Fax: (602) 271-4930

### ARKANSAS

Ms. Lisa DeLoache Melton
Arkansas IOLTA Program
Suite 304
209 W. Capitol Avenue
Little Rock, AR 72201
Telephone: (501) 376-1801
Fax: (501) 376-8266

## CALIFORNIA

Ms. Judy Garlow
Legal Services Trust Fund Program
State Bar of California
555 Franklin Street
San Francisco, CA 94102
Telephone: (415) 561-8252
Fax: (415) 561-8829

## COLORADO

Ms. Meredith McBurney
Colorado Lawyer Trust Account
    Foundation
Suite 950
1900 Grant Street
Denver, CO 80203
Telephone: (303) 863-7221
Fax: (303) 894-0821

## CONNECTICUT

Ms. Sandy F. Klebanoff
Connecticut Bar Foundation IOLTA
    Program
99 Pratt Street
Hartford, CT 06103-1607
Telephone: (860) 722-2494
Fax: (860) 722-2497

Ms. Liz Drummond
Connecticut Bar Foundation IOLTA
    Program
99 Pratt Street
Hartford, CT 06103-1607
Telephone (860) 722-2494
Fax: (860) 722-2497

## DELAWARE

Mr. Bruce M. Stargatt, Esq.
IOLTA for the State of Delaware
Young, Conaway, Stargatt & Taylor

Rodney Square N., P.O. Box 391
Wilmington, DE 19899-0391
Telephone: (302) 571-6614
Fax: (302) 571-1253

Ms. Lucinda Scrimshaw
IOLTA for the State of Delaware
Delaware Bar Foundation
1225 N. King St., 10th Fl.
Wilmington, DE 19801
Telephone: (302) 658-5279
Fax: (302) 658-5212

## DISTRICT OF COLUMBIA

Ms. Deborah R. Jones
District of Columbia Bar Foundation
    IOLTA Program
Suite 700
1700 K Street N.W.
Washington, DC 20006
Telephone: (202) 467-4231
Fax: (202) 775-0008

Ms. Zona Hostetler
District of Columbia Bar Foundation
    IOLTA Program
Suite 700
1700 K Street N.W.
Washington, DC 20006
Telephone: (202) 467-4231
Fax: (202) 775-0008

## FLORIDA

Ms. Jane E. Curran
The Florida Bar Foundation
P.O. Box 1553
Suite 405, 109 E. Church St.
Orlando, FL 32801-9919
Telephone: (407) 843-0045
Fax: (407) 839-0287

Ms. Jeanne Sams
The Florida Bar Foundation
P.O. Box 1553
Suite 405, 109 E. Church St.
Orlando, FL 32801-9919
Telephone: (407) 843-0045
Fax: (407) 839-0287

## GEORGIA

Mr. Len Horton
State Bar of Georgia IOLTA
800 The Hurt Building
Atlanta, GA 30303
Telephone: (404) 527-8765
Fax: (404) 527-8717

## HAWAII

Mr. Peter Adler
Hawaii Justice Foundation
P.O. Box 1936
Suite 645, 810 Richards St.
Honolulu, HI 96813
Telephone: (808) 537-3886
Fax: (808) 528-1974

## IDAHO

Ms. Barbara A. Anderson
Idaho Law Foundation, Inc.
P.O. Box 895
Boise, ID 83701
Telephone: (208) 334-4500
Fax: (208) 334-4515

## ILLINOIS

Ms. Ruth Ann Schmitt
Lawyers Trust Fund of Illinois
Suite 3420
55 E. Monroe Street
Chicago, IL 60603

Telephone: (312) 372-5906
Fax: (312) 372-1962

Mr. Mark Marquardt
Lawyers Trust Fund of Illinois
Suite 3420
55 E. Monroe Street
Chicago, IL 60603
Telephone: (312) 372-5906
Fax: (312) 372-1962

## INDIANA

Mr. David Remondini
Indiana Supreme Court
304 State House
Indianapolis, IN 46204-2798
Fax: (317) 232-8372

## IOWA

Mr. John (S.) Courtney
Iowa Lawyer Trust Account
   Commission
State Capitol
Des Moines, IA 50319
Telephone: (515) 246-8076
Fax: (515) 246-8059

## KANSAS

Mr. Art Thompson
Kansas Bar Foundation
P.O. Box 1037
Topeka, KS 66601
Telephone: (913) 234-5696
Fax: (913) 234-3813

## KENTUCKY

Mr. Jonathan D. Shontz
Kentucky Bar Foundation
514 West Main Street
Frankfort, KY 40601-1883

Telephone: (502) 564-3795
    Extension: 245
Fax: (502) 564-3225

## LOUISIANA

Ms. Linda Dodenhoff
Louisiana Bar Foundation/IOLTA
    Program
601 Saint Charles Avenue
New Orleans, LA 70130
Telephone: (504) 561-1046
Fax: (504) 566-1926

## MAINE

Ms. Joanne D'Arcangelo
Maine Bar Foundation
Suite 201
72 Winthrop Street
Augusta, ME 04330
Telephone: (207) 622-3477
Fax: (207) 623-4140

## MARYLAND

Mr. Robert J. Rhudy
Maryland Legal Services
    Corporation
Suite 102, Charles Towers
15 Charles Plaza
Baltimore, MD 21201
Telephone: (410) 576-9494
Fax: (410) 385-1831

Ms. Susan Erlichman
Maryland Legal Services
    Corp.
222 N. Charles Street
Suite 102
Baltimore, MD 21201
Telephone: (410) 576-9494
Fax: (410) 385-1831

## MASSACHUSETTS

Ms. Jayne Tyrrell
Massachusetts IOLTA
    Committee
Suite 820
11 Beacon Street
Boston, MA 02108-3307
Telephone: (617) 723-9093
Fax: (617) 367-8815

Ms. Kate Guedj
Massachusetts Bar Foundation
20 West Street
Boston, MA 02111-1218
Telephone: (617) 542-3602
    Extension: 300
Fax: (617) 426-4344

Mr. Lonnie A. Powers
Massachusetts Legal Assistance
    Corporation
Suite 820
11 Beacon Street
Boston, MA 02108-3307
Telephone: (617) 367-8544
Fax: (617) 367-8815

Mr. Douglas Havens
Boston Bar Foundation
16 Beacon Street
Boston, MA 02108
Telephone: (617) 742-0615
Fax: (617) 523-0127

## MICHIGAN

Ms. Linda K. Rexer
Michigan State Bar Foundation
306 Townsend Street
Lansing, MI 48933-2083
Telephone: (517) 371-6907
Fax: (517) 371-3325

## MINNESOTA

Ms. Judith L. Rehak
Minnesota Lawyer Trust Account
  Board
135 Minnesota Judicial Center
25 Constitution Avenue
St. Paul, MN 55155
Telephone: (612) 297-7800
Fax: (612) 297-5636

Ms. Nancy Kleeman
Minnesota Volunteer Attorney
  Program
Minnesota Law Center
514 Nicollet Mall, Suite 3
Minneapolis, MN 55402
Telephone: (612) 333-1183

## MISSISSIPPI

Ms. Angie K. Cook
Mississippi Bar Foundation IOLTA
  Program
P.O. Box 2168
Jackson, MS 39225-2168
Telephone: (601) 948-4471
  Extension: 224
Fax: (601) 355-8635

## MISSOURI

Mr. Glenn L. Baker
Missouri Lawyer Trust Account
  Foundation
P.O. Box 63
Jefferson City, MO 65102
Telephone: (314) 634-8117
Fax: (314) 635-4116

## MONTANA

Ms. Judy Williams
State Bar of Montana

P.O. Box 3093
2442 First Avenue N.
Billings, MT 59101
Telephone: (406) 252-6351
Fax: (406) 252-6055

## NEBRASKA

Ms. Doris J. Huffman
Nebraska Lawyers Trust Account
  Foundation
P.O. Box 81809
Lincoln, NE 68501
Telephone: (402) 475-7091
Fax: (402) 475-7098

## NEVADA

Ms. Susan Baucum
Nevada Law Foundation
1833 West Charleston Blvd.
Las Vegas, NV 89102
Telephone: (702) 384-1204
Fax: (702) 384-4149

## NEW HAMPSHIRE

Ms. Lucy C. Metting
New Hampshire Bar Foundation
  IOLTA Program
112 Pleasant Street
Concord, NH 03301
Telephone: (603) 224-6942
Fax: (603) 224-2910

## NEW JERSEY

Ms. Ruth Birkhead
IOLTA Fund of the Bar of New
  Jersey
New Jersey Law Center
One Constitution Square
New Brunswick, NJ 08901-2815

Telephone: (908) 247-8222
Fax: (908) 249-2815

## NEW MEXICO

Ms. Michelle Giger
New Mexico Bar Foundation IOLTA
    Program
P.O. Box 2184
Albuquerque, NM 87103-2184
Telephone: (505) 764-9417
Fax: (505) 242-5179

## NEW YORK

Ms. Lorna Blake
IOLA Fund of the State of New York
Suite 711, The Bar Building
36 W. 44th Street
New York, NY 10036-8100
Telephone: (212) 944-9640
Fax: (212) 944-9836

## NORTH CAROLINA

Mr. Allen Mast
North Carolina State Bar Plan for
    IOLTA
P.O. Box 2687
208 Fayetteville St. Mall
Raleigh, NC 27602-2687
Telephone: (919) 828-0477
Fax: (919) 828-1718

## NORTH DAKOTA

Ms. Sandi Tabor
North Dakota State Bar Foundation,
    Inc.
P.O. Box 2136
Bismarck, ND 58502
Telephone: (701) 255-1404
Fax: (701) 224-1621

## OHIO

Mr. Robert M. Clyde, Jr.
Ohio Legal Assistance Foundation
Suite 420
8 East Long St.
Columbus, OH 43215
Telephone: (614) 752-8919
Fax: (614) 728-3749

## OKLAHOMA

Mr. Tony A. Scott
Oklahoma Bar Foundation
P.O. Box 53036
Oklahoma City, OK 73152
Telephone: (405) 524-2365
Fax: (405) 524-1115

## OREGON

Ms. Ann Bartsch
Oregon Law Foundation
5200 S.W. Meadows Road
Lake Oswego, OR 97035
Telephone: (503) 620-0222
    Extension: 323
Fax: (503) 684-1366

Mr. Rich Cecchetti
Oregon Law Foundation
P.O. Box 1689
Lake Oswego, OR 97035-0889
Telephone: (503) 620-0222
    Extension: 373
Fax: (503) 684-1366

## PENNSYLVANIA

Mr. Alfred J. Azen
Lawyer Trust Account Board
P.O. Box 1025
121 South Street

Harrisburg, PA 17108-1025
Telephone: (717) 238-2001
Fax: (717) 238-2003

## RHODE ISLAND

Ms. Helen D. McDonald
Rhode Island Bar Foundation
    IOLTA Program
115 Cedar Street
Providence, RI 02903
Telephone: (401) 421-6541
Fax: (401) 421-2703

## SOUTH CAROLINA

Mr. Sam M. Pierson, III
South Carolina Bar Foundation
    IOLTA Program
P.O. Box 608
Columbia, SC 29202-0608
Telephone: (803) 765-0517
Fax: (803) 799-4118

## SOUTH DAKOTA

Mr. Thomas C. Barnett, Jr.
South Dakota Bar Foundation
    IOLTA Program
222 East Capitol
Pierre, SD 57501-2596
Telephone: (605) 224-7554
Fax: (605) 224-0282

## TENNESSEE

Ms. Barri E. Bernstein
Tennessee Bar Foundation IOLTA
    Program
Suite 104
214 2nd Ave. North
Nashville, TN 37201

Telephone: (615) 242-1531
Fax: (615) 255-0306

## TEXAS

Mr. LeRoy Cordova
Texas Equal Access To Justice
    Foundation
P.O. Box 12487
400 W. 15th St., Suite 712
Austin, TX 78711
Telephone: (512) 463-1444
Fax: (512) 469-0112

## UTAH

Ms. Zoe A. Brown
Utah Bar Foundation IOLTA
    Program
#204
645 S. 200 East
Salt Lake City, UT 84111-3834
Telephone: (801) 531-9077
Fax: (801) 531-0660

## VERMONT

Ms. Kathleen Stankevich
Vermont Bar Foundation IOLTA
P.O. Box 1170
Montpelier, VT 05601
Telephone: (802) 223-1400
Fax: (802) 223-1573

## VIRGIN ISLANDS

Not Yet Appointed

## VIRGINIA

Mr. Mark Braley
Legal Services Corporation of
    Virginia

Suite 1504
700 E. Maine Street
Richmond, VA 23219
Telephone: (804) 782-9438
Fax: (804) 648-3917

## WASHINGTON

Ms. Barbara C. Clark
Legal Foundation of Washington
Suite 945
500 Union Street
Seattle, WA 98101-2332
Telephone: (206) 624-2536
Fax: (206) 382-3396

## WEST VIRGINIA

Mr. Thomas R. Tinder
West Virginia Bar Foundation
2006 Kanawha Blvd. East
Charleston, WV 25311
Telephone: (304) 558-7993
Fax: (304) 558-2467

## WISCONSIN

Mr. M. Clark Johnson
Wisconsin Trust Account
    Foundation, Inc.

P.O. Box 14197, Suite 105
6441 Enterprise Lane
Madison, WI 53714-0197
Telephone: (608) 273-2595
Fax: (608) 271-4520

## WYOMING

Mr. Jim Tiemann
Wyoming IOLTA Program
Wyoming State Bar Foundation
P.O. Box 109
Cheyenne, WY 82001-0109
Telephone: (307) 632-9061
Fax: (307) 632-3737

Mr. Tony Lewis
Wyoming State Bar Foundation
    IOLTA
P.O. Box 109
500 Randall Avenue
Cheyenne, WY 82003-0109
Telephone: (307) 632-9061
Fax: (307) 632-3737

# INDEX

---

---

# Selected Books From...

# THE SECTION OF LAW PRACTICE MANAGEMENT

**ABA Guide to International Business Negotiations.** A guide to the general, legal, and cultural issues that arise during international negotiations.

**ABA Guide to Legal Marketing.** A collection of new and innovative marketing ideas and strategies for lawyers and firms.

**ABA Guide to Professional Managers in the Law Office.** The book provides guidelines that show how professional management can and does work. It shows lawyers how to practice more efficiently by delegating management tasks to professional managers.

**Becoming Computer Literate.** A guide to computer basics for lawyers and other legal professionals.

**Billing Innovations**. This new book looks at innovative fee arrangements and how your approach toward billing can deeply affect the attorney-client relationship. It also explains how billing and pricing are absolutely intertwined with strategic planning, maintaining quality of services, marketing, instituting a compensation system, and firm governance.

**Changing Jobs, 2nd Ed.** A handbook designed to help lawyers make changes in their professional careers. Includes career planning advice from nearly 50 experts.

**Compensation Plans for Law Firms, 2nd Ed.** This second edition discusses the basics for a fair and simple compensation system for partners, of counsel, associates, paralegals, and staff.

**Do-It-Yourself Public Relations.** A hands-on guide for lawyers with public relations ideas, sample letters and forms. The book includes a diskette that includes model letters to the press that have paid off in news stories and media attention.

**\*\*Finding the Right Lawyer.** A guide that answers the questions people need to ask when searching for legal counsel. It includes a glossary of legal specialties and the ten questions you should ask a lawyer before hiring.

**Flying Solo: A Survival Guide for the Solo Lawyer, 2nd Ed.** An updated and expanded guide to the problems and issues unique to the solo practitioner.

**How to Draft Bills Clients Rush to Pay.** A collection of techniques for drafting bills that project honesty, competence, fairness and value and how draft an inviting statement.

**\*\*How to Get and Keep Good Clients, 2nd ed.** Best-selling author and acknowledged marketing ace Jay Foonberg gives time-proven tips and techniques that you can use for long-range and immediate marketing success.

**\*\*How to Start and Build a Law Practice, 3rd Ed.** Jay Foonberg's classic guide has been updated and expanded. Included are more than 10 new chapters on marketing, financing, automation, practicing from home, ethics and professional responsibility.

**Law Office Staff Manual for Solos and Small Firms.** A book to help solo and small firm practitioners set up their own law office staff manuals. It includes a diskette containing the text of the manual. The diskette is in WordPerfect 5.1 and ASCHII formats.

**Lawyer's Guide to the Internet.** A no-nonsense guide to what the Internet is (and isn't), how it applies to the legal profession, and the different ways it can -- and should -- be used.

**The Lawyer's Guide to Marketing on the Internet.** This book talks about the pluses and minuses of marketing on the Internet, as well as how to develop an Internet marketing plan.

**Leveraging with Legal Assistants.** Reviews the changes that have led to increased use of legal assistants and the need to enlarge their role further. Learn specific ways in which a legal assistant can handle a substantial portion of traditional lawyer work.

**LOCATE, 1995-96.** Co-published with the Association of Legal Administrators. It includes about 140 vendors, 300-400 different software products, and totally revamped listings that will make it easy for you to find the right software.

**Microsoft® Word for Windows in One Hour for Lawyers.** This book includes special tips for users of Windows 95. It contains four easy lessons--timed at 15 minutes each--that will help lawyers prepare, save, and edit a basic document.

**Results-Oriented Financial Management.** A Guide to Successful Law Firm Financial Performance. How to manage "the numbers," from setting rates and computing billable hours to calculating net income and preparing the budget. Over 30 charts and statements to help you prepare reports.

**Survival Guide for Road Warriors: Essential for the Mobile Lawyer.** A guide to using a notebook computer and combinations of equipment and technology so lawyers can be effective in their office, on the road, in the courtroom or at home.

**Through the Client's Eyes: New Approaches to Get Clients to Hire You Again and Again.** Includes an overview of client relations and sample letters, surveys, and self-assessment questions to gauge your client relations acumen.

**TQM in Action: One Firm's Journey Toward Quality and Excellence.** A guide to implementing the principles of Total Quality Management in your law firm.

**Win-Win Billing Strategies.** Represents the first comprehensive analysis of what constitutes "value," and how to bill for it. You'll learn how to initiate and implement different billing methods that make sense for you and your client.

**Women Rainmakers' 101+ Best Marketing Tips.** A collection of over 130 marketing tips suggested by women rainmakers throughout the country. Includes tips on image, networking, public relations, and advertising.

**WordPerfect® 101 for the Law Office.** A book for new users of WordPerfect 6.1. It reviews the basics of WordPerfect--creating, editing and saving documents. Includes exercises on diskette.

**WordPerfect® 201 for the Law Office.** An intermediate course in WordPerfect 6.1. The book delves into advanced editing and automation features. Includes exercises on diskette.

**WordPerfect® 6.1 for Windows in One Hour for Lawyers.** This is a crash course in the most popular word processing software package used by lawyers. In four lessons, you'll learn the basic steps for getting a simple job done.

**WordPerfect® Shortcuts for Lawyers.** A fast-track guide to two of WordPerfect's more advanced functions: merge and macros. Includes 4 lessons designed to take 15 minutes each.

*\*\*Books by Jay G Foonberg*

# Order Form

| Qty | Title | LPM Price | Regular Price | Total |
|-----|-------|-----------|---------------|-------|
| _____ | ABA Guide to Int'l Business Negotiations (511-0331) | $ 74.95 | $ 84.95 | $_____ |
| _____ | ABA Guide to Legal Marketing (511-0341) | 69.95 | 79.95 | $_____ |
| _____ | ABA Guide to Prof. Managers in the Law Office (511-0373) | 69.95 | 79.95 | $_____ |
| _____ | Becoming Computer Literate (511-0342) | 32.95 | 39.95 | $_____ |
| _____ | Billing Innovations (511-0366) | 124.95 | 144.95 | $_____ |
| _____ | Changing Jobs, 2nd Ed. (511-0334) | 49.95 | 59.95 | $_____ |
| _____ | Compensation Plans for Lawyers (511-0353) | 69.95 | 79.95 | $_____ |
| _____ | Do-It-Yourself Public Relations (511-0352) | 69.95 | 79.95 | $_____ |
| _____ | Finding the Right Lawyer (511-0339) | 19.95 | 19.95 | $_____ |
| _____ | Flying Solo, 2nd Ed. (511-0328) | 59.95 | 69.95 | $_____ |
| _____ | How to Draft Bills Clients Rush to Pay (511-0344) | 39.95 | 49.95 | $_____ |
| _____ | How to Get and Keep Good Clients (511-0347) | 99.00 | 99.00 | $_____ |
| _____ | How to Start & Build a Law Practice, 3rd Ed. (511-0293) | 32.95 | 39.95 | $_____ |
| _____ | Law Office Staff Manual for Solos & Small Firms (511-0361) | 49.95 | 59.95 | $_____ |
| _____ | Lawyer's Guide to the Internet (511-0343) | 24.95 | 29.95 | $_____ |
| _____ | Lawyer's Guide to Marketing on the Internet (511-0371) | 54.95 | 64.95 | $_____ |
| _____ | Leveraging with Legal Assistants (511-0322) | 59.95 | 69.95 | $_____ |
| _____ | LOCATE 1995-96 (511-0359) | 65.00 | 75.00 | $_____ |
| _____ | Microsoft Word for Windows in One Hour (511-0358) | 19.95 | 29.95 | $_____ |
| _____ | Survival Guide for Road Warriors (511-0362) | 24.95 | 29.95 | $_____ |
| _____ | Results-Oriented Financial Management (511-0319) | 44.95 | 54.95 | $_____ |
| _____ | Through the Client's Eyes (511-0337) | 69.95 | 79.95 | $_____ |
| _____ | TQM in Action (511-0323) | 59.95 | 69.95 | $_____ |
| _____ | Win-Win Billing Strategies (511-0304) | 89.95 | 99.95 | $_____ |
| _____ | Women Rainmakers' 101+ Best Marketing Tips (511-0336) | 14.95 | 19.95 | $_____ |
| _____ | WordPerfect 101 for the Law Office (511-0364) | 59.95 | 64.95 | $_____ |
| _____ | WordPerfect 201 for the Law Office (511-0365) | 59.95 | 64.95 | $_____ |
| _____ | WordPerfect 101 & 201 Package (511-0339) | 89.90 | 99.90 | $_____ |
| _____ | WordPerfect® 6.1 for Windows in One Hour for Lawyers (511-0354) | 19.95 | 29.95 | $_____ |
| _____ | WordPerfect® Shortcuts for Lawyers (511-0329) | 14.95 | 19.95 | $_____ |

*HANDLING
$ 2.00-$9.99 . . . . . . . . $2.00
10.00-24.99 . . . . . . . . $3.95
25.00-49.99 . . . . . . . . $4.95
50.00 + . . . . . . . . . . . $5.95

**TAX
DC residents add 5.75%
IL residents add 8.75%
MD residents add 5%

SUBTOTAL: $_____
*HANDLING: $_____
**TAX: $_____

TOTAL: $_____

**PAYMENT**

☐ Check enclosed (Payable to the ABA)          ☐ Bill Me

☐ Visa ☐ MasterCard ☐ American Express    Account Number:_____Exp. Date: _____

Signature _____

Name_____

Firm_____

Address_____

City_____State_____ZIP_____

Phone number_____

**Mail to:** ABA, Publication Orders, P.O. Box 10892, Chicago, IL  60610-0892

**Phone:** (312) 988-5522          **Fax:** (312) 988-5568
**Email:** abasvcctr@attmail.com          **World Wide Web:** http//www.abanet.org/lpm/catalog          BOOK

 **THE SECTION OF LAW PRACTICE MANAGEMENT**

# CUSTOMER COMMENT FORM

Title of Book:_____

We've tried to make this publication as useful, accurate, and readable as possible. Please take 5 munutes to tell us if we succeeded. Your comments and suggestions will help us improve our publications. Thank you!

1. How did you acquire this publication:

☐ by mail order        ☐ at a meeting/convention        ☐ as a gift

☐ by phone order       ☐ at a bookstore                 ☐ don't know

☐ other: (describe)_____

Please rate this publication as follows:

|  | Excellent | Good | Fair | Poor | Not Applicable |
|---|---|---|---|---|---|
| **Readability:** Was the book easy to read and understand? | ☐ | ☐ | ☐ | ☐ | ☐ |
| **Examples/Cases:** Were they helpful, practical? Were there enough? | ☐ | ☐ | ☐ | ☐ | ☐ |
| **Content:** Did the book meet your expectations? Did it cover the subject adequately? | ☐ | ☐ | ☐ | ☐ | ☐ |
| **Organization and clarity:** Was the sequence of text logical? Was it easy to find what you wanted to know? | ☐ | ☐ | ☐ | ☐ | ☐ |
| **Illustrations/forms/checklists:** Were they clear and useful? Were there enough? | ☐ | ☐ | ☐ | ☐ | ☐ |
| **Physical attractiveness:** What did you think of the appearance of the publication (typesetting, printing, etc.)? | ☐ | ☐ | ☐ | ☐ | ☐ |

Would you recommend this book to another attorney/administrator?  ☐ Yes ☐ No

How could this publication be improved? What else would you like to see in it?

_____

_____

_____

Do you have other comments or suggestions?_____

_____

_____

Name_____

Firm/Company_____

Address_____

City/State/ZIP_____ Phone_____

Firm Size_____ Area of specialization_____

**We appreciate your time and help.**

**Fold**

NO POSTAGE
NECESSARY
IF MAILED
IN THE
UNITED STATES

# BUSINESS REPLY MAIL
FIRST CLASS       PERMIT NO. 16471       CHICAGO, ILLINOIS

*POSTAGE WILL BE PAID BY ADDRESSEE*

AMERICAN BAR ASSOCIATION
PPM, 8TH FLOOR
750 N. LAKE SHORE DRIVE
CHICAGO, ILLINOIS 60611-9851

**Fold**

AMERICAN BAR ASSOCIATION

## Membership Application

### Access to all these information resources and discounts – for just $2.92 a month!

Membership dues are just $35 a year – just $2.92 a month.
You probably spend more on your general business magazines and newspapers.
But they can't help you succeed in building and managing your practice like LPM.
Make a small investment in success.  Join today!

☑ **Yes!** I want to join the Section of Law Practice Management and gain access to information helping me add more clients, retain and expand business with current clients, and run my law practice more efficiently and competitively!

### Check the dues that apply to you:

❑ $35 for ABA members          ❑ $5 for ABA Law Student Division members

### Choose your method of payment:

❑ Check enclosed (make payable to American Bar Association)
❑ Bill me
❑ Charge to my:     ❑ VISA®      ❑ MASTERCARD®      ❑ AMEX®

Card No.: _____  Exp. Date: _____

Signature: _____  Date: _____

ABA I.D.*: _____
*(∗ Please note: Membership in ABA is a prerequisite to enroll in ABA Sections.)*

Name: _____

Firm/Organization: _____

Address: _____

City/State/ZIP: _____

Telephone No.: _____  Fax No.: _____

Primary Email Address: _____

### Save time by Faxing or Phoning!

▶ Fax your application to:  (312) 988-5820
▶ Join by phone if using a credit card:  (800) 285-2221 (ABA1)
▶ Email us for more information at:  lpm@attmail.com
▶ Check us out on the Internet:  http://www.abanet.org/lpm/org

---

**GUARANTEED SATISFACTION:**
Your membership must save you time, must give you the edge you need to thrive in the increasingly competitive law business – just as it does for our other 20,000 members. However, if for any reason, at anytime, you think we're not working for you, cancel your membership and receive a refund on the unused portion of your membership.

---

*I understand that Section dues include a $24 basic subscription to Law Practice Management; this subscription charge is not deductible from the dues and additional subscriptions are not available at this rate.  Membership dues in the American Bar Association are not deductible as charitable contributions for income tax purposes.  However, such dues may be deductible as a business expense.*

THE SECTION OF
**LAW PRACTICE
MANAGEMENT**

750 N. LAKE SHORE DRIVE
CHICAGO, IL 60611
PHONE: (312) 988-5619
FAX: (312) 988-5820
Email: lpm@attmail.com